WHY MASLOW?

Huntersville, North Carolina, US, April 24, 2018

First published by Juan Rodulfo
Copyright © 2018 by Juan Rodulfo
All rights reserved.
No part of this publication may be reproduced, stored or transmitted in any form or by any means, electronic, mechanical, photocopying, recording, scanning or otherwise without written permission from the publisher. It is illegal to copy this book, publish it on a website, or distribute it by any other means without permission.
Juan Rodulfo has no responsibility for the persistence or accuracy of URLs of external or third-party Internet websites referenced in this publication and does not warrant that the content of such websites is, or will remain, accurate or appropriate.
The names used by companies to distinguish their products are often claimed as trademarks. All trademarks and product names used in this book and on its cover, trade names, service marks, trademarks are trademarks of their respective owners. The publishers and the book are not associated with any products or suppliers mentioned in this book.
None of the companies or organizations referenced in the book have endorsed it.
Library of Congress Catalog
Names: Rodulfo, Juan
ISBN: 979-8-3305-3430-2 (paperback)
ISBN: 979-8-3305-3429-6 (e-book)
ISBN: 979-8-3305-3431-9 (hardcover)
First edition
Layout by Juan Rodulfo
Cover art by Juan Rodulfo
Production: Aussie Trading, LLC
books@aussietrading.ltd
Printed in the USA

Aussie Trading

whymaslow.com

"Before a student's cognitive needs can be met, they must first fulfill their basic physiological needs. For example, a tired and hungry student will find it difficult to focus on learning. Students need to feel emotionally and physically safe and accepted within the classroom to progress and reach their full potential."

whymaslow.com

whymaslow.com

CONTENT

PREFACE 11
PART I. THE MASLOW THEORY 13
   Who was Abraham Maslow? 15
   Maslow's Hierarchy of Needs 19
      The original hierarchy of needs five-stage model
      includes: 22
      Maslow posited that human needs are arranged in a
      hierarchy: 24
      Hierarchy of needs summary 25
      The expanded hierarchy of needs 25
      Self-actualization 27
      Maslow offers the following description of self-
      actualization: 28
      Characteristics of self-actualized people 28
      Characteristics of self-actualizers: 29
      Behavior leading to self-actualization: 30
   Different approaches 37
      Methodology 38
      Ranking 39
         Global ranking 39
         Ranking of sex 39
         Changes to the hierarchy by circumstance 40
      Definition of terms 42
         Self-actualization 42
         Human or non-human needs 42
   Educational applications 43
   A Practical Approach to Maslow's Hierarchy of Needs 44
      Basic Human Needs Continuum 45
PART II. GOVERNMENTS AND THE HIERARCHY OF
NEEDS 47
   Food, Water, Shelter, Sleep 49
      Food Security 49
      Measurement 52
      Rates 55

- Examples of food insecurity 55
- Food security by country 56
  - Afghanistan 56
  - Mexico 56
  - United States 57
  - Democratic Republic of Congo 58
- Growth of World Food Supply (caloric base) per capita 59
  - Availability 60
  - Access 61
  - Utilization 62
  - Stability 63
  - Effects of food insecurity 64
  - Stunting and chronic nutritional deficiencies 64
- Challenges to achieving food security 66
  - Global water crisis 66
  - Land degradation 68
  - Climate change 68
  - Agricultural diseases 71
  - Food versus fuel 71
  - Politics 72
  - Food sovereignty 74
- Children and food security 75
  - In the United States 75
  - Gender and food security 78
- Homelessness 81
  - Here are his five top reasons why homelessness in America is the black sheep of politics: 88
- Health, Family, Social Stability 91
  - Health inequalities 97
  - Health determinants 98
  - Citizenship 98
- Education 101
  - How Education and Training Affect the Economy. 104
  - How much extra productivity would he or she expect to gain? 107

Barriers to Education around the World 109
   A lack of funding for education 109
   Having no teacher, or having an untrained teacher. 110
   No classroom 111
   A lack of learning materials 112
   The exclusion of children with disabilities 112
   Being the 'wrong' gender 113
   Living in a country in conflict or at risk of conflict 114
   Distance from home to school 115
   Hunger and poor nutrition 116
   The expense of education 117
PART III. GOVERNMENTS AND THE HIERARCHY OF NEEDS 119
   Keep them on their primitive stage! 121
      Proposed Operational Definitions of Deprivation of Basic Human Need for Youth 122
THE AUTHOR 133
   Publications: 134
      Books: 134
      Blogs: 134
   Audiovisual Productions: 135
      Podcasts: 135
      Music: 135
      Photography & Video: 135
   Social Media Profiles: 135
Endnotes 137

PREFACE

It was my second year of studies at the University by 1988-1989, when I first studied Abraham Harold Maslow, since then his theory has served me as a tool to construe the different environments where I have been playing different roles as Human, Son, Brother, Friend, Leader, Worker, Father and all the other roles the Society has given me.

After getting graduated, and have faced the realities of the Career in my country, I knew that the only way to claim this Pyramid for me was to become into an Entrepreneur, of course once taking impulse from the Government Help to buy a home (Shelter 1st Pyramid Stage) and get Loan to pay my Master Degree Studies (Education/Esteem Needs 4th Pyramid Stage), once claimed this stages, I was prepared to reach the last Stage, but something happened, Political Forces[i] suddenly and violently kicked me and my family (along with hundreds more) away from the 4th Maslow Pyramid of Needs Stage to the primitive Stage 1, forced to ride cities, towns looking for groceries or medicine, afraid of being kidnapped, robbed or incarcerated by criminals or the Government itself, through their paramilitary forces or Armed and Police Forces corrupted again under the Government supervision.

This fear pushed me far away landing into the US to seek shelter, food, water, security, safety and friends, back in Spot 1…

Enjoying infinite meditation moments as Landscape then Junker Worker, Delivery Truck and LYFT Driver, was able to study this civilization from the First World[ii], most of the people lives over the 1st and 2nd Stages of the Pyramid of Needs, because the Government/Private Sector with all its deficiencies has been able to provide to most of their citizens with shelter, food, water, security and safety.

Why Maslow? He came again to my mind, because I realized that his Theory is the vivid structure of our society, in any of its Worlds: First, Second, Third, etc., in this book I try to understand the world framing it with his Pyramid of Needs, with the hope of a World were the ones of the top help the ones on the ground for real…LOL! What is real is that any of you that read this book will be able to Understand his/her situation and will claim the Pyramid not over the head of others but helping the ones on lower stages to claim it! This would be the best Halloween for the 20% of the population that actually owns the pinnacle over the rest of Us.

PART I. THE MASLOW THEORY

1

Who was Abraham Maslow?

Abraham Maslow was a psychologist concerned with the nature of human experience; that is a humanistic psychologist. In 1943 he proposed a theory that described the different needs that all humans have and the hierarchy in which those needs are organized. According to Maslow, the higher-level needs cannot be satisfied unless the lower-level needs have been met. This hierarchy has had a significant impact on the field of psychology and education as well[iii].

Abraham Harold Maslow was born April 1, 1908, in Brooklyn, New York. He was the first of seven children born to his parents, who themselves were uneducated Jewish immigrants from Russia. His parents, hoping for the best for their children in the new world, pushed him hard for academic success. Not surprisingly, he became very lonely as a boy and found his refuge in books.

To satisfy his parents, he first studied law at the City College of New York (CCNY). After three semesters, he transferred to Cornell, and then back to CCNY. He married Bertha Goodman, his first cousin, against his parent's wishes. Abe and Bertha went on to have two daughters.

He and Bertha moved to Wisconsin so that he could attend the University of Wisconsin. Here, he became interested in psychology, and his schoolwork began to improve dramatically. He spent time there working with Harry Harlow, who is famous for his experiments with baby rhesus monkeys and attachment behavior.

He received his BA in 1930, his MA in 1931, and his PhD in 1934, all in psychology, all from the University of Wisconsin. A year after graduation, he returned to New York to work with E. L. Thorndike at Columbia, where Maslow became interested in research on human sexuality.

He began teaching full time at Brooklyn College. During this period of his life, he came into contact with the many European intellectuals that were immigrating to the US, and Brooklyn in particular, at that time -- people like Adler, Fromm, Horney, as well as several Gestalt and Freudian psychologists.

Maslow served as the chair of the psychology department at Brandeis from 1951 to 1969. While there he met Kurt Goldstein, who had originated the idea of self-actualization in his famous book, The Organism (1934). It was also here that he began his crusade for a humanistic psychology -- something ultimately much more important to him than his own theorizing.

He spent his final years in semi-retirement in California, until, on June 8, 1970, he died of a heart attack after years of ill health.[iv]

whymaslow.com

2

Maslow's Hierarchy of Needs

One of the many interesting things Maslow noticed while he worked with monkeys early in his career was that some needs take precedence over others. For example, if you are hungry and thirsty, you will tend to try to take care of the thirst first. After all, you can do without food for weeks, but you can only do without water for a couple of days! Thirst is a "stronger" need than hunger. Likewise, if you are very very thirsty, but someone has put a choke hold on you and you can't breathe, which is more important? The need to breathe, of course. On the other hand, sex is less powerful than any of these. Let's face it, you won't die if you don't get it![v]

Maslow's hierarchy of needs is a motivational theory in psychology comprising a five-tier model of human needs, often depicted as hierarchical levels within a pyramid.

Needs lower down in the hierarchy must be satisfied before individuals can attend to needs higher up. From the bottom of the hierarchy upwards, the needs are physiological, safety, love and belonging, esteem and self-actualization.

This five-stage model can be divided into deficiency needs and growth needs. The first four levels are often referred to as deficiency needs (D-needs), and the top level is known as growth or being needs (B-needs).

Deficiency needs arise due to deprivation and are said to motivate people when they are unmet. Also, the motivation to fulfill such needs will become stronger the longer the duration they are denied. For example, the longer a person goes without food, the hungrier they will become.

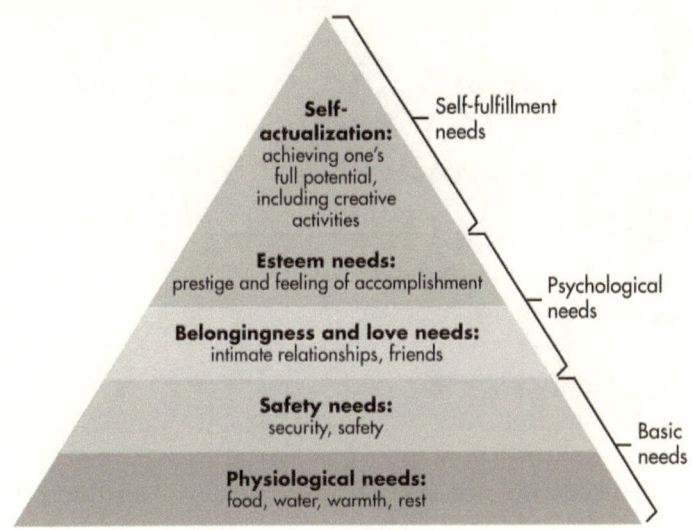

Deficiency needs vs. growth needs.

Maslow (1943) initially stated that individuals must satisfy lower-level deficit needs before progressing on to meet higher level growth needs. However, he later clarified that satisfaction of a need is not an "all-or-none" phenomenon, admitting that his earlier statements may have given "the false impression that a need must be satisfied 100 percent before the next need emerges" (1987, p. 69).

When a deficit need has been 'more or less' satisfied it will go away, and our activities become habitually directed towards meeting the next set of needs that we have yet to satisfy. These then become our salient needs. However, growth needs continue to be felt and may even become stronger once they have been engaged.

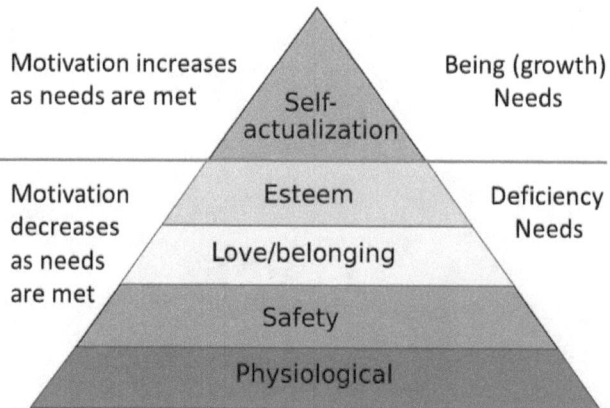

Growth needs do not stem from a lack of something, but rather from a desire to grow as a person. Once this growth needs have been reasonably satisfied, one may be able to reach the highest level called self-actualization.

Every person is capable and has the desire to move up the hierarchy toward a level of self-actualization. Unfortunately, progress is often disrupted by a failure to meet lower-level needs. Life experiences, including divorce and loss of a job, may cause an individual to fluctuate between levels of the hierarchy.

Therefore, not everyone will move through the hierarchy in a unidirectional manner but may move back and forth between the different types of needs.

The original hierarchy of needs five-stage model includes:

Maslow (1943, 1954) stated that people are motivated to achieve certain needs and that some needs take precedence over others. Our most basic need is for physical survival, and this will be the first thing that motivates our behavior. Once that level is fulfilled the next level up is what motivates us, and so on.

1. Physiological needs - these are biological requirements for human survival, e.g. air, food, drink, shelter, clothing, warmth, sex, sleep.

If these needs are not satisfied the human body cannot function optimally. Maslow considered physiological needs the most important as all the other needs become secondary until these needs are met.

2. Safety needs - protection from elements, security, order, law, stability, freedom from fear.

3. Love and belongingness needs - after physiological and safety needs have been fulfilled, the third level of human needs is social and involves feelings of belongingness. The need for interpersonal relationships motivates behavior.

Examples include friendship, intimacy, trust, and acceptance, receiving and giving affection and love. Affiliating, being part of a group (family, friends, work).

4. Esteem needs - which Maslow classified into two categories: (i) esteem for oneself (dignity, achievement, mastery, independence) and (ii) the desire for reputation or respect from others (e.g., status, prestige).

Maslow indicated that the need for respect or reputation is most important for children and adolescents and precedes real self-esteem or dignity.

5. Self-actualization needs - realizing personal potential, self-fulfillment, seeking personal growth and peak experiences. A desire "to become everything one is capable of becoming" (Maslow, 1987, p. 64).

Maslow posited that human needs are arranged in a hierarchy:

"It is quite true that man lives by bread alone — when there is no bread. But what happens to man's desires when there is plenty of bread and when his belly is chronically filled?

At once other (and "higher") needs emerge and these, rather than physiological hungers, dominate the organism. And when these in turn are satisfied, again new (and still "higher") needs emerge and so on. This is what we mean by saying that the basic human needs are organized into a hierarchy of relative prepotency" (Maslow, 1943, p. 375).

Maslow continued to refine his theory based on the concept of a hierarchy of needs over several decades (Maslow, 1943, 1962, 1987).

Regarding the structure of his hierarchy, Maslow (1987) proposed that the order in the hierarchy "is not nearly as rigid" (p. 68) as he may have implied in his earlier description.

Maslow noted that the order of needs might be flexible based on external circumstances or individual differences. For example, he notes that for some individuals, the need for self-esteem is more important than the need for love. For others, the need for creative fulfillment may supersede even the most basic needs.

Maslow (1987) also pointed out that most behavior is multi-motivated and noted that "any behavior tends to be determined by several or all of the basic needs simultaneously rather than by only one of them" (p. 71).

Hierarchy of needs summary

(a) Human beings are motivated by a hierarchy of needs.

(b) needs are organized in a hierarchy of prepotency in which more basic needs must be more or less met (rather than all or none) prior to higher needs.

(c) The order of needs is not rigid but instead may be flexible based on external circumstances or individual differences.

(d) Most behavior is multi-motivated, that is, simultaneously determined by more than one basic need.

The expanded hierarchy of needs

It is important to note that Maslow's (1943, 1954) five-stage model has been expanded to include cognitive and aesthetic needs (Maslow, 1970a) and later transcendence needs (Maslow, 1970b).

Changes to the original five-stage model are highlighted and include a seven-stage model and an eight-stage model; both developed during the 1960's and 1970s.

1. Biological and physiological needs - air, food, drink, shelter, warmth, sex, sleep, etc.

2. Safety needs - protection from elements, security, order, law, stability, etc.

3. Love and belongingness needs - friendship, intimacy, trust, and acceptance, receiving and giving affection and love. Affiliating, being part of a group (family, friends, work).

4. Esteem needs - which Maslow classified into two categories: (i) esteem for oneself (dignity, achievement, mastery, independence) and (ii) the desire for reputation or respect from others (e.g., status, prestige).

5. Cognitive needs - knowledge and understanding, curiosity, exploration, need for meaning and predictability.

6. Aesthetic needs - appreciation and search for beauty, balance, form, etc.

7. Self-actualization needs - realizing personal potential, self-fulfillment, seeking personal growth and peak experiences.

8. Transcendence needs - A person is motivated by values which transcend beyond the personal self (e.g., mystical experiences and certain experiences with nature, aesthetic

experiences, sexual experiences, service to others, the pursuit of science, religious faith, etc.).

Self-actualization

Instead of focusing on psychopathology and what goes wrong with people, Maslow (1943) formulated a more positive account of human behavior which focused on what goes right. He was interested in human potential, and how we fulfill that potential.

Psychologist Abraham Maslow (1943, 1954) stated that human motivation is based on people seeking fulfillment and change through personal growth. Self-actualized people are those who were fulfilled and doing all they were capable of.

The growth of self-actualization (Maslow, 1962) refers to the need for personal growth and discovery that is present throughout a person's life. For Maslow, a person is always 'becoming' and never remains static in these terms. In self-actualization, a person comes to find a meaning to life that is important to them.

As each individual is unique, the motivation for self-actualization leads people in different directions (Kenrick et al., 2010). For some people self-actualization can be achieved through creating works of art or literature, for others through sport, in the classroom, or within a corporate setting.

Maslow (1962) believed self-actualization could be measured through the concept of peak experiences. This occurs when a person experiences the world totally for what it is, and there are feelings of euphoria, joy, and wonder.

It is important to note that self-actualization is a continual process of becoming rather than a perfect state one reaches of a 'happy ever after' (Hoffman, 1988).

Maslow offers the following description of self-actualization:

'It refers to the person's desire for self-fulfillment, namely, to the tendency for him to become actualized in what he is potentially.

The specific form that these needs will take will of course vary greatly from person to person. In one individual it may take the form of the desire to be an ideal mother, in another it may be expressed athletically, and in still another it may be expressed in painting pictures or in inventions' (Maslow, 1943, p. 382–383).

Characteristics of self-actualized people

Although we are all, theoretically, capable of self-actualizing, most of us will not do so, or only to a limited degree. Maslow (1970) estimated that only two percent of people would reach the state of self-actualization. He was especially interested in the characteristics of people whom he considered to have achieved their potential as individuals.

By studying 18 people he considered to be self-actualized (including Abraham Lincoln and Albert Einstein) Maslow (1970) identified 15 characteristics of a self-actualized person.

Characteristics of self-actualizers:

1. They perceive reality efficiently and can tolerate uncertainty.
2. Accept themselves and others for what they are.
3. Spontaneous in thought and action.
4. Problem-centered (not self-centered).
5. Unusual sense of humor.
6. Able to look at life objectively.
7. Highly creative.
8. Resistant to enculturation, but not purposely unconventional.
9. Concerned for the welfare of humanity.
10. Capable of deep appreciation of basic life-experience.
11. Establish deep satisfying interpersonal relationships with a few people.
12. Peak experiences.
13. Need for privacy.
14. Democratic attitudes.
15. Strong moral/ethical standards.

Behavior leading to self-actualization:

(a) Experiencing life like a child, with full absorption and concentration.

(b) Trying new things instead of sticking to safe paths.

(c) Listening to your own feelings in evaluating experiences instead of the voice of tradition, authority or the majority.

(d) Avoiding pretense ('game playing') and being honest.

(e) Being prepared to be unpopular if your views do not coincide with those of the majority.

(f) Taking responsibility and working hard.

(g) Trying to identify your defenses and having the courage to give them up.

The characteristics of self-actualizers and the behaviors leading to self-actualization are shown in the list above. Although people achieve self-actualization in their own unique way, they tend to share certain characteristics. However, self-actualization is a matter of degree, 'There are no perfect human beings' (Maslow,1970a, p. 176).

It is not necessary to display all 15 characteristics to become self-actualized, and not only self-actualized people will display them. Maslow did not equate self-actualization with perfection. Self-actualization merely involves achieving one's potential. Thus, someone can be silly, wasteful, vain and impolite, and still self-actualize. Less than two percent of the population achieves self-actualization.[vi]

In his influential paper of 1943, A Theory of Human Motivation, the American psychologist Abraham Maslow proposed that healthy human beings have a certain number of needs, and that these needs are arranged in a hierarchy, with some needs (such as physiological and safety needs) being more primitive or basic than others (such as social and ego needs). Maslow's so-called 'hierarchy of needs' is often presented as a five-level pyramid, with higher needs coming into focus only once lower, more basic needs are met.

Maslow called the bottom four levels of the pyramid 'deficiency needs' because a person does not feel anything if they are met but becomes anxious if they are not. Thus, physiological needs such as eating, drinking, and sleeping are deficiency needs, as are safety needs, social needs such as friendship and sexual intimacy, and ego needs such as self-esteem and recognition. In contrast, Maslow called the fifth level of the pyramid a 'growth need' because it enables a person to 'self-actualize' or reach his fullest potential as a human being. Once a person has met his deficiency needs, he can turn his attention to self-actualization; however, only a small minority of people is able to self-actualize because self-actualization requires uncommon qualities such as honesty, independence, awareness, objectivity, creativity, and originality.

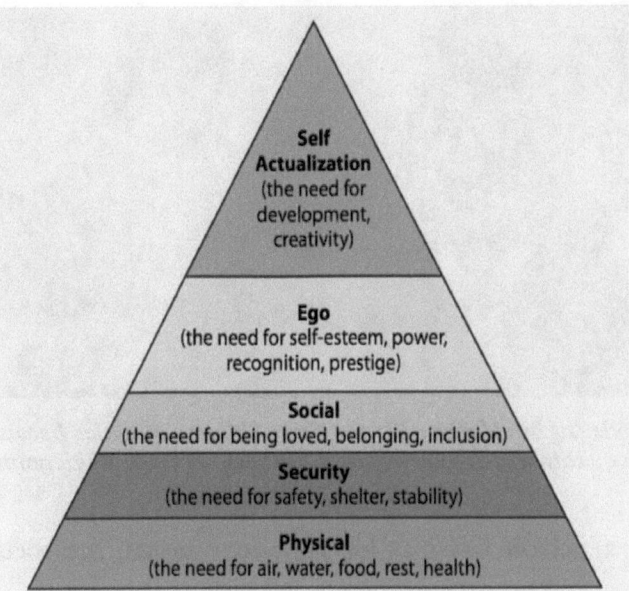

Maslow's Hierarchy of Needs, Source: Neel Burton

Although Maslow's hierarchy of needs has been criticized for being overly schematic and lacking in scientific grounding, it presents an intuitive and potentially useful theory of human motivation. After all, there is surely some grain of truth in the popular saying that one cannot philosophize on an empty stomach, and in Aristotle's early observation that 'all paid work absorbs and degrades the mind'.

Aristotle (right): 'Courage is the first of human qualities because it is the quality which guarantees the others.' Source: Wikicommons

Once a person has met his deficiency needs, the focus of his anxiety shifts to self-actualization and he begins—even if only at a subconscious or semiconscious level—to contemplate the context and meaning of life. He may come to fear that death in inevitable and that life is meaningless, but at the same time cling on to the cherished belief that his life is eternal or at least important. This gives rise to an inner conflict that is sometimes referred to as 'existential anxiety' or, more colorfully, as 'the trauma of non-being'.

Existential anxiety is so disturbing that most people avoid it at all costs. They construct an inauthentic but comforting reality made up of moral codes, bourgeois values, habits, customs, culture, and even— arguably—religion. The Harvard theologian Paul Tillich (1886-1965) and indeed Freud himself suggested that religion is nothing more than a carefully crafted coping mechanism for existential anxiety. For Tillich true faith consists simply in 'being vitally concerned with that ultimate reality to which I give the symbolical name of God.'

According to the philosopher Jean-Paul Sartre (1905-1980), by refusing to face up to 'non-being' a person is acting in 'bad faith', and so living out a life that is inauthentic and unfulfilling. Facing up to non-being can bring a sense of calm, freedom, even nobility and—yes—it can also bring insecurity, loneliness, responsibility, and consequently anxiety. But far from being pathological, this anxiety is a sign of health, strength, and courage. As Freud noted, 'Most people do not really want freedom, because freedom involves responsibility, and most people are frightened of responsibility.'

For Tillich, refusing to face up to non-being not only leads to a life that is inauthentic, but also to neurotic anxiety. Tillich witheringly remarked that neurosis is 'the way of avoiding non-being by avoiding being'. According to this outlook, neurotic anxiety arises from repressed existential anxiety, which itself arises from the nature of the human condition and, more specifically, from our uniquely human capacity for self-consciousness.

Facing up to non-being enables a person to put his life into perspective, see it in its entirety, and thereby give it a sense of direction and unity. If the ultimate source of anxiety is a fear of the future, the future ends in death; and if the ultimate source of anxiety is uncertainty, death is the only certainty. Facing up to death, accepting its inevitability, and integrating it into life not only cures one of neurosis, but also enables one to get and make the most out of life.[vii]

3

Different approaches

What is human nature? Are there innate, hierarchical, human needs and motivations? Have they transformed? What are the social-political implications? Over seventy years ago Abraham Maslow submitted "A Theory of Human Motivation" (1943). His subsequent pyramid-shape hierarchy of needs captured the world's imagination by suggesting that humans are driven by innate needs for survival, safety, love and belonging, esteem, and self-realization, in that order.

Nearly all academic works eventually fall into oblivion, some instantaneously. One third of social science articles go utterly uncited (Remler 2014). Some pieces, however, do outlive their authors, and continue to live in the minds of their peers and followers. Think of Thomas Kuhn's The Structure of Scientific Revolutions, which currently leads the list of most cited works in the social sciences and the humanities, followed by Everett Rogers' Diffusion of Innovations, Paulo Freire' Pedagogy of the Oppressed, and Michael Porter's Competitive Strategy (Green 2016). Have you read, or at least heard of, all four? If not, you are in good company. Even the most cited works often remain obscure beyond their designated field, and almost all are unknown beyond academia.

The fate of Maslow's hierarchy of human needs is different. It has resonated powerfully in scholarship across disciplines. More interestingly, it remains, some 75 years after its articulation, well known beyond the ivory tower. Whenever I try to introduce Maslow's pyramid to first-year students, I quickly realize it needs no introduction. They have heard of it, have seen some popularized versions of it, before, and it struck a chord. Instinctively, it feels familiar. The continued resonance of Maslow's theory in popular imagination, however unscientific it may seem, is possibly the single most telling evidence of its significance: *it explains human nature as something that most humans immediately recognize in themselves and others.*[viii]

Methodology

Maslow studied what he called the master race of people such as Albert Einstein, Jane Addams, Eleanor Roosevelt, and Frederick Douglass rather than mentally ill or neurotic people, writing that "the study of crippled, stunted, immature, and unhealthy specimens can yield only a cripple psychology and a cripple philosophy." Maslow studied the healthiest 1% of the college student population.

Ranking

Global ranking

In their extensive review of research based on Maslow's theory, Wahba and Bridwell found little evidence for the ranking of needs that Maslow described or for the existence of a definite hierarchy at all.

The order in which the hierarchy is arranged has been criticized as being ethnocentric by Geert Hofstede. Maslow's hierarchy of needs fails to illustrate and expand upon the difference between the social and intellectual needs of those raised in individualistic societies and those raised in collectivist societies. The needs and drives of those in individualistic societies tend to be more self-centered than those in collectivist societies, focusing on improvement of the self, with self-actualization being the apex of self-improvement. In collectivist societies, the needs of acceptance and community will outweigh the needs for freedom and individuality.

Ranking of sex

The position and value of sex on the pyramid has also been a source of criticism regarding Maslow's hierarchy. Maslow's hierarchy places sex in the physiological needs category along with food and breathing; it lists sex solely from an individualistic perspective. For example, sex is placed with other physiological needs which must be satisfied before a person considers "higher" levels of motivation. Some critics feel this placement of sex neglects the emotional, familial, and evolutionary implications of sex within the community, although others point out that this is true of all of the basic needs.

Changes to the hierarchy by circumstance

The higher-order (self-esteem and self-actualization) and lower-order (physiological, safety, and love) needs classification of Maslow's hierarchy of needs is not universal and may vary across cultures due to individual differences and availability of resources in the region or geopolitical entity/country.

In one study, exploratory factor analysis (EFA) of a thirteen-item scale showed there were two particularly important levels of needs in the US during the peacetime of 1993 to 1994: survival (physiological and safety) and psychological (love, self-esteem, and self-actualization). In 1991, a retrospective peacetime measure was established and collected during the Persian Gulf War and US citizens were asked to recall the importance of needs from the previous year. Once again, only two levels of needs were identified; therefore, people have the ability and competence to recall and estimate the importance of needs. For citizens in the Middle East (Egypt and Saudi

Arabia), three levels of needs regarding importance and satisfaction surfaced during the 1990 retrospective peacetime. These three levels were completely different from those of the US citizens.

Changes regarding the importance and satisfaction of needs from the retrospective peacetime to the wartime due to stress varied significantly across cultures (the US vs. the Middle East). For the US citizens, there was only one level of needs since all needs were considered equally important. With regards to satisfaction of needs during the war, in the US there were three levels: physiological needs, safety needs, and psychological needs (social, self-esteem, and self-actualization). During the war, the satisfaction of physiological needs and safety needs were separated into two independent needs while during peacetime, they were combined as one. For the people of the Middle East, the satisfaction of needs changed from three levels to two during wartime.

A 1981 study looked at how Maslow's hierarchy might vary across age groups. A survey asked participants of varying ages to rate a set number of statements from most important to least important. The researchers found that children had higher physical need scores than the other groups, the love need emerged from childhood to young adulthood, the esteem need was highest among the adolescent group, young adults had the highest self-actualization level, and old age had the highest level of security, it was needed across all levels comparably. The authors argued that this suggested Maslow's hierarchy may be limited as a theory for developmental sequence since the sequence of the love need and the self-esteem need should be reversed according to age.

Definition of terms
Self-actualization

The term "self-actualization" may not universally convey Maslow's observations; this motivation refers to focusing on becoming the best person that one can possibly strive for in the service of both the self and others. (non-primary source needed) Maslow's term of self-actualization might not properly portray the full extent of this level; quite often, when a person is at the level of self-actualization, much of what they accomplish in general may benefit others, or "the greater good".

Human or non-human needs

Abulof argues that while Maslow stresses that "motivation theory must be anthropocentric rather than animal-centric", his theory erects a largely animalistic pyramid, crowned with a human edge: "Man's higher nature rests upon man's lower nature, needing it as a foundation and collapsing without this foundation… Our godlike qualities rest upon and need our animal qualities." Abulof notes that "all animals seek survival and safety, and many animals, especially mammals, also invest efforts to belong and gain esteem... The first four of Maslow's classical five rungs feature nothing exceptionally human." Even when it comes to "self-actualization," Abulof argues, it is unclear how distinctively human is the actualizing "self." After all, the latter, according to Maslow, constitutes "an inner, more biological, more instinctual core of human nature," thus "the search for one's own intrinsic, authentic values" checks the human freedom of choice: "A musician must make music," so freedom is limited to merely the choice of instrument.[ix]

Educational applications[x]

Maslow's (1962) hierarchy of needs theory has made a major contribution to teaching and classroom management in schools. Rather than reducing behavior to a response in the environment, Maslow (1970a) adopts a holistic approach to education and learning. Maslow looks at the complete physical, emotional, social, and intellectual qualities of an individual and how they impact learning.

Applications of Maslow's hierarchy theory to the work of the classroom teacher are obvious. Before a student's cognitive needs can be met, they must first fulfill their basic physiological needs. For example, a tired and hungry student will find it difficult to focus on learning. Students need to feel emotionally and physically safe and accepted within the classroom to progress and reach their full potential.

Maslow suggests students must be shown that they are valued and respected in the classroom, and the teacher should create a supportive environment. Students with low self-esteem will not progress academically at an optimum rate until their self-esteem is strengthened.

Maslow (1971, p. 195) argued that a humanistic educational approach would develop people who are "stronger, healthier, and would take their own lives into their hands to a greater extent. With increased personal responsibility for one's personal life, and with a rational set of values to guide one's choosing, people would begin to actively change the society in which they lived".

A Practical Approach to Maslow's Hierarchy of Needs

The reality is that in daily life, most of us are pursuing all of these human needs simultaneously to varying degrees. Instead of focusing on which need you're attempting to meet, consider the overall direction of your life.

Instead of stacking the needs, one on top of the other, psychologist Clayton Alderfer, illustrated them on a horizontal continuum.

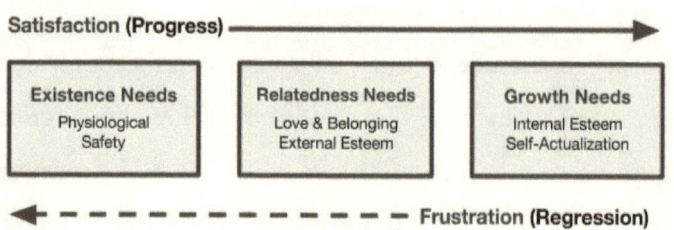

Basic Human Needs Continuum

If you're investing an increasing effort in your growth, you probably feel more satisfied. And this satisfaction will likely fuel your growth efforts further.

Research by psychologist Martin Seligman confirms this. Seligman, the founder of positive psychology, finds that people feel more gratification (lasting happiness) when they are pursuing growth by playing to their natural strengths.

If, however, your emphasis is turning to unmet relatedness and existence needs, your frustration is building. Frustration diminishes your motivation to grow.[xi]

PART II. GOVERNMENTS AND THE HIERARCHY OF NEEDS

4

Food, Water, Shelter, Sleep

"Before a student's cognitive needs can be met, they must first fulfill their basic physiological needs. For example, a tired and hungry student will find it difficult to focus on learning. Students need to feel emotionally and physically safe and accepted within the classroom to progress and reach their full potential."

Food Security

"There are three traditional routes to national food security: 1) domestic production, which contributes to self-sufficiency; 2) commercial food imports; and 3) international food aid". Therefore, we need to make it clear that there is a distinction "between self-sufficiency and food security, in that the former is only one possible route to food security at the national level". Since 2007/2008, multiple Middle Eastern and North African (MENA) region governments have begun to consider more domestic food production as a part of their national aggregate food security laws. Although from a political view that approach may be justified due to it helping in stabilizing domestic food prices and deducting vulnerability to international markets and reliance on other countries, it comes at an enormous economic cost. This due to the resource endowments of the majority "of MENA countries—water scarcity and lack of arable land—are not well-suited to food production", specifically cereal production, and "these countries' comparative international advantages lie in other economic activities". Many of "the international organizations involved in the MENA economies during the 1990s and the 2000s advocated a food security strategy for most countries" that based on diversifying away from agriculture towards multiple other activities, "including manufacturing exports, with the resulting foreign exchange used to purchase food imports". "Within the agricultural sector there has also been emphasis on shifting resources into high- value crops that are most efficient in water use, such as fruits, vegetables, and tree crops", with a view on export markets, in replace of cereal production for domestic consumption.[xii]

Food security is a condition related to the availability of food, and individuals' accessibility and affordability to it. There is evidence of being in use over 10,000 years ago, with central authorities in civilizations ancient China and ancient Egypt being known to release food from storage in times of famine. At the 1974 World Food Conference the term "food security" was defined with an emphasis on supply. Food security, they said, is the "availability at all times of adequate, nourishing, diverse, balanced and moderate world food supplies of basic foodstuffs to sustain a steady expansion of food consumption and to offset fluctuations in production and prices". Later definitions added demand and access issues to the definition. The final report of the 1996 World Food Summit states that food security "exists when all people, at all times, have physical and economic access to sufficient, safe and nutritious food to meet their dietary needs and food preferences for an active and healthy life".

Household food security exists when all members, at all times, have access to enough food for an active, healthy life. Individuals who are food secure do not live in hunger or fear of starvation. Food insecurity, on the other hand, is a situation of "limited or uncertain availability of nutritionally adequate and safe foods or limited or uncertain ability to acquire acceptable foods in socially acceptable ways", according to the United States Department of Agriculture (USDA). Food security incorporates a measure of resilience to future disruption or unavailability of critical food supply due to various risk factors including droughts, shipping disruptions, fuel shortages, economic instability, and wars. In the years 2011–2013, an estimated 842 million people were suffering from chronic hunger. The Food and Agriculture Organization of the United Nations, or FAO, identified the four pillars of food security as availability, access, utilization, and stability.

The United Nations (UN) recognized the Right to Food in the Declaration of Human Rights in 1948 and has since noted that it is vital for the enjoyment of all other rights.

The 1996 World Summit on Food Security declared that "food should not be used as an instrument for political and economic pressure". According to the International Centre for Trade and Sustainable Development, failed agriculture market regulation and the lack of anti-dumping mechanisms cause much of the world's food scarcity and malnutrition.

Measurement

Food security can be measured by calorie intake per person per day, available on a household budget. In general, the objective of food security indicators and measures is to capture some or all of the main components of food security in terms of food availability, access and utilization or adequacy. While availability (production and supply) and utilization/adequacy (nutritional status/anthropometric measures) seemed much easier to estimate, thus more popular, access (ability to acquire sufficient quantity and quality) remained largely elusive. The factors influencing household food access are often context specific.

Several measures have been developed that aim to capture the access component of food security, with some notable examples developed by the USAID-funded Food and

Nutrition Technical Assistance (FANTA) project, collaborating with Cornell and Tufts University and Africare and World Vision. These include:

- Household Food Insecurity Access Scale (HFIAS) – continuous measure of the degree of food insecurity (access) in the household in the previous month
- Household Dietary Diversity Scale (HDDS) – measures the number of different food groups consumed over a specific reference period (24hrs/48hrs/7days).
- Household Hunger Scale (HHS)- measures the experience of household food deprivation based on a set of predictable reactions, captured through a survey and summarized in a scale.
- Coping Strategies Index (CSI) – assesses household behaviors and rates them based on a set of varied established behaviors on how households cope with food shortages. The methodology for this research is based on collecting data on a single question: "What do you do when you do not have enough food, and do not have enough money to buy food?"

Food insecurity is measured in the United States by questions in the Census Bureau's Current Population Survey. The questions asked are about anxiety that the household budget is inadequate to buy enough food, inadequacy in the quantity or quality of food eaten by adults and children in the household, and instances of reduced food intake or consequences of reduced food intake for adults and for children. A National Academy of Sciences study commissioned by the USDA criticized this measurement and the relationship of "food security" to hunger, adding "it is not clear whether hunger is appropriately identified as the extreme end of the food security scale."

The FAO, World Food Programme (WFP), and International Fund for Agricultural Development (IFAD) collaborate to produce The State of Food Insecurity in the World. The 2012 edition described improvements made by the FAO to the prevalence of undernourishment (PoU) indicator that is used to measure rates of food insecurity. New features include revised minimum dietary energy requirements for individual countries, updates to the world population data, and estimates of food losses in retail distribution for each country. Measurements that factor into the indicator include dietary energy supply, food production, food prices, food expenditures, and volatility of the food system. The stages of food insecurity range from food secure situations to full-scale famine. A new peer-reviewed journal, Food Security: The Science, Sociology and Economics of Food Production and Access to Food, began publishing in 2009.

Rates

With its prevalence of undernourishment (PoU) indicator, the FAO reported that almost 870 million people were chronically undernourished in the years 2010–2012. This represents 12.5% of the global population,

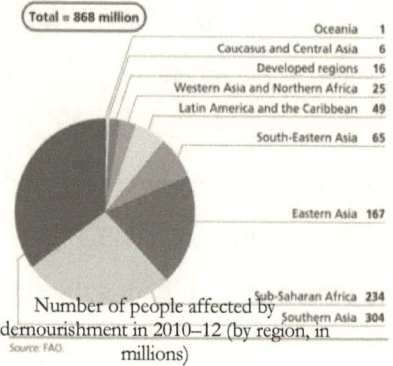

Number of people affected by undernourishment in 2010–12 (by region, in millions)
Source: FAO.

or 1 in 8 people. Higher rates occur in developing countries, where 852 million people (about 15% of the population) are chronically undernourished. The report noted that Asia and Latin America have achieved reductions in rates of undernourishment that put these regions on track for achieving the Millennium Development Goal of halving the prevalence of undernourishment by 2015. The UN noted that about 2 billion people do not consume a sufficient amount of vitamins and minerals. In India, the second-most populous country in the world, 30 million people have been added to the ranks of the hungry since the mid-1990s and 46% of children are underweight.

Examples of food insecurity

Famines have been frequent in world history. Some have killed millions and substantially diminished the population of a large area. The most common causes have been drought and war, but the greatest famines in history were caused by economic policy.

Food security by country

Afghanistan

In Afghanistan about 35% of households are food insecure. The prevalence of underweight, stunting, and wasting in children under 5 years of age is also very high.

Mexico

Food insecurity has distressed Mexico throughout its history and continues to do so in the present. Food availability is not the issue; rather, severe deficiencies in the accessibility of food contribute to the insecurity. Between 2003 and 2005, the total Mexican food supply was well above the sufficient to meet the requirements of the Mexican population, averaging 3,270 kilocalories per daily capita, higher than the minimum requirements of 1,850 kilocalories per daily capita. However, at least 10 percent of the population in every Mexican state suffers from inadequate food access. In nine states, 25–35 percent lives in food-insecure households. More than 10 percent of the populations of seven Mexican states fall into the category of Serious Food Insecurity.

The issue of food inaccessibility is magnified by chronic child malnutrition as well as obesity in children, adolescents, and family.

Mexico is vulnerable to drought which can further cripple agriculture.

United States

The United States Department of Agriculture defines food insecurity as "limited or uncertain availability of nutritionally adequate and safe foods or limited or uncertain ability to acquire acceptable foods in socially acceptable ways." Food security is defined by the USDA as "access by all people at all times to enough food for an active, healthy life."

National Food Security Surveys are the main survey tool used by the USDA to measure food security in the United States. Based on respondents' answers to survey questions, the household can be placed on a continuum of food security defined by the USDA. This continuum has four categories: high food security, marginal food security, low food security, and very low food security. Economic Research Service report number 155 (ERS-155) estimates that 14.5 percent (17.6 million) of US households were food insecure at some point in 2012. The prevalence of food insecurity has been relatively in the United States since the economic recession 2008.

In 2016:

12.3 percent (15.6 million) of U.S. households were food insecure at some time during 2016.

7.4 percent (9.4 million) of U.S. households had low food security in 2016.

4.9 percent (6.1 million) of U.S. households had very low food security at some time during 2016.

Both children and adults were food insecure in 8.0 percent of households with children (3.1 million households).

Democratic Republic of Congo

The Democratic Republic of Congo is the second largest country in Africa; the country is dealing with food insecurity. Although they have an abundance of natural resources, they lack accessibility of essential foods makes it difficult for the Congolese people in their daily lives. Malnutrition is high among children affects their ability, and children who live in a rural area are affected more than children who are live in an urban area. In the Democratic Republic of Congo, about 33% of households are food insecure; it is 60% in eastern provinces. A study showed the correlation of food insecurity negatively affecting at-risk HIV adults in the Democratic Republic of Congo.

In 2007-2008 grain prices increased and the people in the Democratic Republic of the Congo went to civil unrest, there were riots and protest. Hunger is frequent in this country, but sometimes it is to the extreme that many families cannot afford to eat every day. Bushmeat trade was used to measure the trend of food security. The trend signifies the amount of consumption in urban and rural areas. Urban areas mainly consume bush meat because they cannot afford other types of meat.

The Rome Declaration called for the members of the United Nations to work to halve the number of chronically undernourished people on the Earth by the year 2015. The Plan of Action sets a number of targets for government and non-governmental organizations for achieving food security, at the individual, household, national, regional and global levels.

Another World Summit on Food Security took place at the FAO's headquarters in Rome between November 16 and 18, 2009. The decision to convene the summit was taken by the Council of FAO in June 2009, at the proposal of FAO Director-General Dr Jacques Diouf. Heads of state and government attended this summit.

Growth of World Food Supply (caloric base) per capita

The WHO states that there are three pillars that determine food security: food availability, food access, and food use and misuse. The FAO adds a fourth pillar: the stability of the first three dimensions of food security over time. In 2009, the

World Summit on Food Security stated that the "four pillars of food security are availability, access, utilization, and stability".

Availability

Food availability relates to the supply of food through production, distribution, and exchange. Food production is determined by a variety of factors including land ownership and use; soil management; crop selection, breeding, and management; livestock breeding and management; and harvesting. Crop production can be affected by changes in rainfall and temperatures. The use of land, water, and energy to grow food often competes with other uses, which can affect food production. Land used for agriculture can be used for urbanization or lost to desertification, salinization, and soil erosion due to unsustainable agricultural practices. Crop production is not required for a country to achieve food security. Nations don't have to have the natural resources required to produce crops in order to achieve food security, as seen in the examples of Japan and Singapore.

Because food consumers outnumber producers in every country, food must be distributed to different regions or nations. Food distribution involves the storage, processing, transport, packaging, and marketing of food. Food-chain infrastructure and storage technologies on farms can also affect the amount of food wasted in the distribution process. Poor transport infrastructure can increase the price of supplying water and fertilizer as well as the price of moving food to national and global markets. Around the world, few individuals or households are continuously self-reliant for food. This creates the need for a bartering, exchange, or cash economy to acquire food. The exchange of food requires efficient trading systems and market institutions, which can affect food security. Per capita world food supplies are more than adequate to provide food security to all, and thus food accessibility is a greater barrier to achieving food security.

Access

Food access refers to the affordability and allocation of food, as well as the preferences of individuals and households. The UN Committee on Economic, Social, and Cultural Rights noted that the causes of hunger and malnutrition are often not a scarcity of food but an inability to access available food, usually due to poverty. Poverty can limit access to food and can also increase how vulnerable an individual or household is to food price spikes. Access depends on whether the household has enough income to purchase food at prevailing prices or has sufficient land and other resources to grow its own food. Households with enough resources can overcome unstable harvests and local food shortages and maintain their access to food.

There are two distinct types of access to food: direct access, in which a household produces food using human and material resources, and economic access, in which a household purchases food produced elsewhere. Location can affect access to food and which type of access a family will rely on. The assets of a household, including income, land, products of labor, inheritances, and gifts can determine a household's access to food. However, the ability to access sufficient food may not lead to the purchase of food over other materials and services. The demographics and education levels of members of the household as well as the gender of the household head determine the preferences of the household, which influences the type of food that is purchased. A household's access to enough and nutritious food may not assure adequate food intake of all household members, as intra household food allocation may not sufficiently meet the requirements of each member of the household. The USDA adds that access to food must be available in socially acceptable ways, without, for example, resorting to emergency food supplies, scavenging, stealing, or other coping strategies.

Utilization

The next pillar of food security is food utilization, which refers to the metabolism of food by individuals. Once food is obtained by a household, a variety of factors affect the quantity and quality of food that reaches members of the household. In order to achieve food security, the food ingested must be safe and must be enough to meet the physiological requirements of each individual. Food safety affects food utilization, and can be affected by the preparation, processing, and cooking of food in the community and household. Nutritional values of the household determine food choice, and whether food meets cultural preferences is important to utilization in terms of psychological and social well-being. Access to healthcare is another determinant of food utilization, since the health of individuals controls how the food is metabolized. For example, intestinal parasites can take nutrients from the body and decrease food utilization. Sanitation can also decrease the occurrence and spread of diseases that can affect food utilization. Education about nutrition and food preparation can affect food utilization and improve this pillar of food security.

Stability

Food stability refers to the ability to obtain food over time. Food insecurity can be transitory, seasonal, or chronic. In transitory food insecurity, food may be unavailable during certain periods of time. At the food production level, natural disasters and drought result in crop failure and decreased food availability. Civil conflicts can also decrease access to food.

Instability in markets resulting in food-price spikes can cause transitory food insecurity. Other factors that can temporarily cause food insecurity are loss of employment or productivity, which can be caused by illness. Seasonal food insecurity can result from the regular pattern of growing seasons in food production.

Chronic (or permanent) food insecurity is defined as the long-term, persistent lack of adequate food. In this case, households are constantly at risk of being unable to acquire food to meet the needs of all members. Chronic and transitory food insecurity are linked, since the reoccurrence of transitory food security can make households more vulnerable to chronic food insecurity.

Effects of food insecurity

Famine and hunger are both rooted in food insecurity. Chronic food insecurity translates into a high degree of vulnerability to famine and hunger; ensuring food security presupposes elimination of that vulnerability.

Stunting and chronic nutritional deficiencies

Many countries experience ongoing food shortages and distribution problems. These result in chronic and often widespread hunger amongst significant numbers of people. Human populations can respond to chronic hunger and malnutrition by decreasing body size, known in medical terms as stunting or stunted growth. This process starts in the uterus if the mother is malnourished and continues through approximately the third year of life. It leads to higher infant and child mortality, but at rates far lower than during famines. Once stunting has occurred, improved nutritional intake after the age of about two years is unable to reverse the damage. Stunting itself can be viewed as a coping mechanism, bringing body size into alignment with the calories available during adulthood in the location where the child is born. Limiting body size as a way of adapting to low levels of energy (calories) adversely affects health in three ways:

- Premature failure of vital organs during adulthood. For example, a 50-year-old individual might die of heart failure because his/her heart suffered structural defects during early development.
- Stunted individuals suffer a higher rate of disease and illness than those who have not undergone stunting.
- Severe malnutrition in early childhood often leads to defects in cognitive development. It therefore creates disparity among children who did not experience severe malnutrition and those who experience it.

Challenges to achieving food security.

Global water crisis

Water deficits, which are already spurring heavy grain imports in numerous smaller countries, may soon do the same in larger countries, such as China or India. The water tables are falling in scores of countries (including northern China, the US, and India) due to widespread over-pumping using powerful diesel and electric pumps. Other countries affected include Pakistan, Afghanistan, and Iran. This will eventually lead to water scarcity and cutbacks in grain harvest. Even with the over-pumping of its aquifers, China is developing a grain deficit. When this happens, it will almost certainly drive grain prices upward. Most of the 3 billion people projected to be born worldwide by mid-century will be born in countries already experiencing water shortages. After China and India, there is a second tier of smaller countries with large water deficits – Afghanistan, Algeria, Egypt, Iran, Mexico, and Pakistan. Four of these already import a large share of their grain. Only Pakistan remains self-sufficient. But with a population expanding by 4 million a year, it will likely soon turn to the world market for grain.

Regionally, Sub-Saharan Africa has the largest number of water-stressed countries of any place on the globe, as of an estimated 800 million people who live in Africa, 300 million live in a water-stressed environment. It is estimated that by 2030, 75 million to 250 million people in Africa will be living in areas of high-water stress, which will likely displace anywhere between 24 million and 700 million people as conditions become increasingly unlivable. Because the majority of Africa remains dependent on an agricultural lifestyle and 80 to 90 percent of all families in rural Africa rely upon producing their own food, water scarcity translates to a loss of food security.

Multimillion-dollar investments beginning in the 1990s by the World Bank have reclaimed desert and turned the Ica Valley in Peru, one of the driest places on earth, into the largest supplier of asparagus in the world. However, the constant irrigation has caused a rapid drop in the water table, in some places as much as eight meters per year, one of the fastest rates of aquifer depletion in the world. The wells of small farmers and local people are beginning to run dry and the water supply for the main city in the valley is under threat. As a cash crop, asparagus has provided jobs for local people, but most of the money goes to the buyers, mainly the British. A 2010 report concluded that the industry is not sustainable and accuses investors, including the World Bank, of failing to take proper responsibility for the effect of their decisions on the water resources of poorer countries. Diverting water from the headwaters of the Ica River to asparagus fields has also led to a water shortage in the mountain region of Huancavelica, where indigenous communities make a marginal living herding.

Land degradation

Intensive farming often leads to a vicious cycle of exhaustion of soil fertility and decline of agricultural yields. Approximately 40 percent of the world's agricultural land is seriously degraded. In Africa, if current trends of soil degradation continue, the continent might be able to feed just 25 percent of its population by 2025, according to UNU's Ghana-based Institute for Natural Resources in Africa.

Climate change

Extreme events, such as droughts and floods, are forecast to increase as climate change and global warming takes hold. Ranging from overnight floods to gradually worsening droughts, these will have a range of effects on the agricultural sector. According to the Climate & Development Knowledge Network Report Managing Climate Extremes and Disasters in the Agriculture Sectors: Lessons from the IPCC SREX Report, the effects will include changing productivity and livelihood patterns, economic losses, and effects on infrastructure, markets and food security. Food security in future will be linked to our ability to adapt agricultural systems to extreme events. An example of a shifting weather pattern would be a rise in temperatures. As temperatures rise due to climate change there is a risk of a diminished food supply due to heat damage.

Approximately 2.4 billion people live in the drainage basin of the Himalayan rivers. India, China, Pakistan, Afghanistan, Bangladesh, Nepal and Myanmar could experience floods followed by severe droughts in coming decades. In India alone, the Ganges provides water for drinking and farming for more than 500 million people. The west coast of North America, which gets much of its water from glaciers in mountain ranges such as the Rocky Mountains and Sierra Nevada, also would be affected. Glaciers aren't the only worry that the developing nations have; sea level is reported to rise as climate change progresses, reducing the amount of land available for agriculture.

In other parts of the world, a big effect will be low yields of grain according to the World Food Trade Model, specifically in the low latitude regions where much of the developing world is located. From this the price of grain will rise, along with the developing nations trying to grow the grain. Due to this, every 2–2.5% price hike will increase the number of hungry people by 1%. Low crop yields are just one of the problems facing farmers in the low latitudes and tropical regions. The timing and length of the growing seasons, when farmers plant their crops, are going to be changing dramatically, per the USDA, due to unknown changes in soil temperature and moisture conditions.

"Results show that climate change is likely to reduce agricultural production, thus reducing food availability" (Brown etal., 2008.) "The food security threat posed by climate change is greatest for Africa, where agricultural yields and per capita food production has been steadily declining, and where population growth will double the demand for food, water, and livestock forage in the next 30 years" (Devereux et al., 2004).In 2060, the hungry population could range from 641 million to 2087 million with climate change (Chen et al., 1994). By the year 2030, Cereal crops will decrease from 15 to 19 percent; temperatures are estimated to rise from 1 degree Celsius to 2.75 degrees Celsius, which will lead to less rainfall, which will all result in an increase in food insecurity in 2030 (Devereux etal, 2004). In prediction farming countries will be the worst sectors hit, hot countries and drought countries will reach even higher temperatures, and richer countries will be hit the least as they have more access to more resources (Devereux et al. 2004). From a food security perspective, climate change is the dominant rationale to the increase in recent years and predicted years to come.

Agricultural diseases

Diseases affecting livestock or crops can have devastating effects on food availability especially if there are no contingency plans in place. For example, Ug99, a lineage of wheat stem rust which can cause up to 100% crop losses, is present in wheat fields in several countries in Africa and the Middle East and is predicted to spread rapidly through these regions and possibly further afield, potentially causing a wheat production disaster that would affect food security worldwide.

The genetic diversity of the crop wild relatives of wheat can be used to improve modern varieties to be more resistant to rust. In their centers of origin wild wheat plants are screened for resistance to rust, then their genetic information is studied, and finally wild plants and modern varieties are crossed through means of modern plant breeding in order to transfer the resistance genes from the wild plants to the modern varieties.

Food versus fuel

Farmland and other agricultural resources have long been used to produce non-food crops including industrial materials such as cotton, flax, and rubber; drug crops such as tobacco and opium, and biofuels such as firewood, etc. In the 21st century the production of fuel crops has increased, adding to this diversion. However, technologies are also developed to commercially produce food from energy such as natural gas and electrical energy with tiny water and land footprints.

Politics

Nobel Prize winning economist Amartya Sen observed that "there is no such thing as an apolitical food problem." While drought and other naturally occurring events may trigger famine conditions, it is government action or inaction that determines its severity, and often even whether or not a famine will occur. The 20th century has examples of governments, as in Collectivization in the Soviet Union or the Great Leap Forward in the People's Republic of China undermining the food security of their own nations. Mass starvation is frequently a weapon of war, as in the blockade of Germany, the Battle of the Atlantic, and the blockade of Japan during World War I and World War II and in the Hunger Plan enacted by Nazi Germany.

Governments sometimes have a narrow base of support, built upon cronyism and patronage. Fred Cuny pointed out in 1999 that under these conditions: *"The distribution of food within a country is a political issue. Governments in most countries give priority to urban areas, since that is where the most influential and powerful families and enterprises are usually located. The government often neglects subsistence farmers and rural areas in general. The more remote and underdeveloped the area the less likely the government will be to effectively meet its needs. Many agrarian policies, especially the pricing of agricultural commodities, discriminate against rural areas. Governments often keep prices of basic grains at such artificially low levels that subsistence producers cannot accumulate enough capital to make investments to improve their production. Thus, they are effectively prevented from getting out of their precarious situation."*

Dictators and warlords have used food as a political weapon, rewarding supporters while denying food supplies to areas that oppose their rule. Under such conditions food becomes a currency with which to buy support and famine becomes an effective weapon against opposition

Governments with strong tendencies towards kleptocracy can undermine food security even when harvests are good. When government monopolizes trade, farmers may find that they are free to grow cash crops for export, but under penalty of law only able to sell their crops to government buyers at prices far below the world market price. The government then is free to sell their crop on the world market at full price, pocketing the difference.

When the rule of law is absent, or private property is non-existent, farmers have little incentive to improve their productivity. If a farm becomes noticeably more productive than neighboring farms, it may become the target of individuals well connected to the government. Rather than risk being noticed and possibly losing their land, farmers may be content with the perceived safety of mediocrity.

As pointed out by William Bernstein in The Birth of Plenty: "Individuals without property are susceptible to starvation, and it is much easier to bend the fearful and hungry to the will of the state. If a [farmer's] property can be arbitrarily threatened by the state, that power will inevitably be employed to intimidate those with divergent political and religious opinions."

Food sovereignty

The approach known as food sovereignty views the business practices of multinational corporations as a form of neocolonialism. It contends that multinational corporations have the financial resources available to buy up the agricultural resources of impoverished nations, particularly in the tropics. They also have the political clout to convert these resources to the exclusive production of cash crops for sale to industrialized nations outside of the tropics, and in the process to squeeze the poor off of the more productive lands. Under this view subsistence farmers are left to cultivate only lands that are as marginal in terms of productivity as to be of no interest to the multinational corporations. Likewise, food sovereignty holds it to be true that communities should be able to define their own means of production, and that food is a basic human right. With several multinational corporations now pushing agricultural technologies on developing countries, technologies that include improved seeds, chemical fertilizers, and pesticides, crop production has become an increasingly analyzed and debated issue. Many communities calling for food sovereignty are protesting the imposition of Western technologies on to their indigenous systems and agency.

Children and food security

On April 29, 2008, a UNICEF UK report found that the world's poorest and most vulnerable children are being hit the hardest by climate change. The report, "Our Climate, Our Children, Our Responsibility: The Implications of Climate Change for the World's Children", says that access to clean water and food supplies will become more difficult, particularly in Africa and Asia.

In the United States

By way of comparison, in one of the largest food producing countries in the world, the United States, approximately one out of six people are "food insecure", including 17 million children, according to the U.S. Department of Agriculture. A 2012 study in the Journal of Applied Research on Children found that rates of food security varied significantly by race, class and education. In both kindergarten and third grade, 8% of the children were classified as food insecure, but only 5% of white children were food insecure, while 12% and 15% of black and Hispanic children were food insecure, respectively. In third grade, 13% of black and 11% of Hispanic children are food insecure compared to 5% of white children. There are also striking regional variations in food security. Although food insecurity can be difficult to measure, 45% of elementary and secondary students in Maine qualify for free or reduced-price school lunch; by some measures Maine has been declared the most food-insecure of the New England states. Transportation challenges and distance are common barriers to families in rural areas who seek food assistance. Social stigma is another important consideration, and for children, sensitively administering in-school programs can make the difference between success and failure. For instance, when John Woods, co-founder of Full Plates, Full Potential, learned that embarrassed students were shying away from the free breakfasts being distributed at a school he was working with, he made arrangements to provide breakfast free of charge to all of the students there.

According to a 2015 Congressional Budget Office report on child nutrition programs, it is more likely that food insecure children will participate in school nutrition programs than children from food secure families. School nutrition programs, such as the National School Lunch Program (NSLP) and the School Breakfast Program (SBP) have provided millions of children access to healthier lunch and breakfast meals, since their inceptions in the mid-1900s. According to the Centers for Disease Control and Prevention, NSLP has served over 300 million, while SBP has served about 10 million students each day. Nevertheless, far too many qualifying students still fail to receive these benefits simply due to not submitting the necessary paperwork. Multiple studies have reported that school nutrition programs play an important role in ensuring students are accessing healthy meals. Students who ate school lunches provided by NLSP showed higher diet quality than if they had their own lunches. Even more, the USDA improved standards for school meals, which ultimately lead to positive impacts on children's food selection and eating habits.

Countless partnerships have emerged in the quest for food security. A number of federal nutrition programs exist to provide food specifically for children, including the Summer Food Service Program, Special Milk Program (SMP) and Child and Adult Care Food Program (CACFP), and community and state organizations often network with these programs. The Summer Food Program in Bangor, Maine, is run by the Bangor Housing Authority and sponsored by Good Shepherd Food Bank. In turn, Waterville Maine's Thomas College, for example, is among the organizations holding food drives to collect donations for Good Shepherd. Children whose families qualify for Supplemental Nutrition Assistance Program (SNAP) or Women, Infants, and Children (WIC) may also receive food assistance. WIC alone served approximately 7.6 million participants, 75% of which were children and infants.

Despite the sizable populations served by these programs, Conservatives have regularly targeted these programs for defunding. Conservatives' arguments against school nutrition programs include fear of wasting food and fraud from applications. On January 23, 2017, H.R.610 was introduced to the House by Republican Representative Steve King. The bill seeks to repeal a rule set by the Food and Nutrition Service of the Department of Agriculture, which mandates schools to provide more nutritious and diverse foods across the food plate. Two months later, the Trump administration released a preliminary 2018 budget that proposed a $2 billion cut from WIC.

Food insecurity in children can lead to developmental impairments and long-term consequences such as weakened physical, intellectual and emotional development.

Food insecurity is also related to obesity for people living in neighborhoods where nutritious food is unavailable or unaffordable.

Gender and food security

Gender inequality both leads to and is a result of food insecurity. According to estimates women and girls make up 60% of the world's chronically hungry and little progress has been made in ensuring the equal right to food for women enshrined in the Convention on the Elimination of All Forms of Discrimination against Women. Women face discrimination both in education and employment opportunities and within the household, where their bargaining power is lower. Women's employment is essential for not only advancing gender equality within the workforce but ensuring a sustainable future as it means less pressure for high birth rates and net migration. On the other hand, gender equality is described as instrumental to ending malnutrition and hunger. Women tend to be responsible for food preparation and childcare within the family and are more likely to spend their income on food and their children's needs. Women also play an important role in food production, processing, distribution and marketing. They often work as unpaid family workers, are involved in subsistence farming and represent about 43% of the agricultural labor force in developing countries, varying from 20% in Latin America to 50% in Eastern and Southeastern Asia and Sub-Saharan Africa. However, women face discrimination in access to land, credit, technologies, finance and other services. Empirical studies suggest that if women had the same access to productive resources as men, women could boost their yields by 20–30%, raising the overall agricultural output in developing countries by 2.5 to 4%. While those are rough estimates, the significant benefit of closing the gender gap on agricultural productivity cannot be denied. The gendered aspects of food security are visible along the four pillars of food security: availability, access, utilization and stability, as defined by the Food and Agriculture Organization. The number of people affected by hunger is extremely high, with enormous effects on women and girls. Making this trend disappear "must be a top priority for governments and international institutions". Actions governments take must take into consideration that food insecurity is an issue regarding "equality, rights and social justice". "Food and nutrition insecurity is a political and economic phenomenon fueled by inequitable global and national processes". Factors like capitalism, exploration of Indigenous lands all contribute to food insecurity for minorities and the people who are the most oppressed in various countries (women being one of these oppressed groups). To emphasis, "food and nutrition insecurity is a gender justice issue". The facts that women and girls are the most oppressed by "the inequitable global economic processes that govern food systems and by global trends such as climate change", shows how institutions continue to place women in positions of disadvantage and impoverishment to make money and thrive on capitalizing the food system. When the government withholds food by raising its prices to amounts only privileged people can afford, they both benefit and are able to control the "lower class"/ marginalized people via the food market. An interesting fact is that "despite rapid economic growth in India, thousands of women and girls still lack food and nutrition security as a direct result of their lower status compared with men and boys". "Such inequalities are compounded by women and girls' often limited access to productive resources, education and decision-making, by the 'normalized' burden of unpaid work – including care work – and by the endemic problems of gender-based violence (GBV), HIV and AIDS".[xiii]

Homelessness

Homelessness is a complex social problem with a variety of underlying economic and social factors such as poverty, lack of affordable housing, uncertain physical and mental health, addictions, and community and family breakdown. These factors, in varying combinations, contribute to duration, frequency, and type of homelessness. To be fully homeless is to live without shelter; however, many experience partial homelessness that can include uncertain, temporary, or sub-standard shelter. Homelessness is difficult to define, thus governments struggle with uncertainty when creating and implementing policies they hope will effectively manage or eradicate this problem.

Levels of government, in countries like Canada, add to the complexity of dealing with homelessness. Being governed at three different levels, federal, provincial, and municipal, requires high levels of agreement to effectively create and administer policies. In Canada, each level of government is responsible for different facets of homelessness. The federal government, responsible for the whole of Canada, creates and administers policies and funding for aboriginal peoples (a segment of Canada's population over-represented in homeless counts), seniors, and social housing, as well as transfers funds to the provinces to help pay for their social programs. The provincial government, responsible for needs of the provinces and territories, creates and administers policies regarding mental illness, addictions, welfare, minimum wage laws, landlord and tenant acts, and child protection services and shares responsibility with the federal government for seniors and social housing. The municipal governments are seen as the hands or arms of the provincial government, and are technically not responsible for homelessness; however, are often involved in choosing sites for social housing, supporting emergency shelters and hospital emergency wards, as well as providing support, in a variety of ways, to facilitate these initiatives. The fact that there is no comprehensive national housing strategy to co-ordinate these levels of government often lead to inadequate policies and funding that fall far short of meeting the country's housing needs. This lack of coordination towards policy and funding for homelessness has recently come to the attention of courts in Canada who have begun to make decisions which support shelter as an essential right for Canadians. The UN Special Rapporteur on adequate housing in Canada has also strongly urged the federal government to commit sufficient funding to create a national housing strategy by working with the provinces and territories.[xiv]

In an article published by Melanie Onn in The Guardian on September 13th, 2017, titled: **"Homelessness is not inevitable. It's a political choice made by the UK government"**, she found that: "More and more people are starting to notice rising levels of homelessness, as they see rough sleepers on the streets of towns and cities across the country. The reality is that these visible signs of homelessness are just the tip of the iceberg. The new report from the independent National Audit Office (NAO) finds that there are now approximately 4,100 people sleeping rough each year, with 120,000 children living in temporary accommodation.

The scale of the problem now extends to sections of society that go far beyond what people might imagine. On a recent visit to a Crisis center, I heard about a woman who completed her tax return on a laptop from her sleeping bag outside a train station.

whymaslow.com

Perhaps the most troubling conclusion from the NAO's report is that the government doesn't appear to be interested in solving this growing problem. Incredibly, the department with responsibility for preventing homelessness has not yet produced a plan for preventing homelessness.

Welfare reform, including the freeze on housing benefits, is one of the main drivers of homelessness, but the government hasn't bothered to measure its effect. I fear that ministers know what the answers will be, and so don't want to ask the questions.[xv]

In the US, **Homelessness** represents both a policy problem and a political quandary in the United States. In the wealthiest economy in the world, the fact that individuals and families lack housing and must live on the streets, in their cars, or in congregate shelters calls into question the basic functioning of the social safety net and suggests that something is deeply wrong with the political and economic priorities of the country. Yet the dominant discourse in the United States proposes that at least some percentages of homeless people are at fault for their situations; their dysfunctional behavior, aberrant choices, and lack of a work ethic explain their homelessness more than economic inequalities or policy priorities. Within this framework of contrasting views on homelessness, debates rage over the significance of the homeless problem, the reasons people lose their housing, how best to assist them, and who should be classified as homeless. These questions often are linked to one another; why homelessness occurs, and which demographic variables are stressed in describing homeless populations relate directly to whether and how policy is structured to help people become housed.

A relatively invisible political issue affecting a small portion of the population until the early 1980s, homelessness became increasingly problematic throughout the late twentieth and early twenty-first centuries in the United States. Although the economy rose and dipped during these decades, as did the percentage of people living in poverty, homelessness appeared to be a relatively intractable problem. The numbers of people newly homeless generally have not abated, even during periods of economic growth. Still more concerning, the homeless population contains sizable numbers of children and young people, both accompanied by parents and unaccompanied by adults. Most estimates indicate that families with children comprise 30% to 36% of the homeless population (Bassuk et al. 2014; Weinreb, Rog, and Henderson 2010). And the number of homeless children is increasing. Approximately 1.6 million school-aged children were homeless during the

2011–2012 school year: "These numbers represent a 10% increase over the previous school year—an historic high" (Bassuk et al. 2014, 457; National Center on Family Homelessness 2011). As the analysis of policy approaches below suggests, political and policy choices may explain, at least in part, the growing numbers of children who are homeless.

Research indicates that the reasons for homelessness are complicated and multilayered. First and foremost, homelessness is a product of poverty:

A variety of complex social system dislocations—an increasing rate of poverty, a deteriorating social "safety net," the steady loss of low-skill employment and low-income housing, and others—have created a situation … where some people are essentially destined to become homeless. In so many words, we now have more poor and otherwise marginalized people than we have affordable housing in which to accommodate them. (Wright et al. 1998, 6). While the official US poverty rate has hovered around 15% since 2010, estimates suggest that "a third of all people were near poor and poor" in the United States (Iceland 2013, 44). In addition, approximately 6.6% of households have an income below 50% of the poverty line (Iceland 2013, 44), or roughly

$12,000 annually for a family of four, suggesting that the depth of poverty presents a tremendous barrier to housing stability for a considerable portion of the population. As Edin and Shaefer discovered in their research on impoverished families in the United States, approximately 1.5 million households lived on cash incomes of at most $2 per day per person in 2011, a calculation that includes cash welfare payments but does not include in-kind assistance like food programs (Edin and Shaefer 2015). ***When poverty is that profound, people clearly struggle to afford basic necessities such as housing, food, clothing, and utilities and are at considerable risk of becoming homeless.*** [xvi]

Joel John Roberts published online: A recent Canadian survey asked their local political candidates to share their position on housing, shelter, and homelessness. Only one-third of them responded.

Are we surprised at the lack of response?

Here in America, homelessness has exploded in the past few decades. Yes, in recent years, chronic homelessness (those people who have struggled on our streets the longest) is being reduced through an innovative approach that immediately houses homeless people.

But the sad fact in America is that on any given night nearly three-quarters of a million people are homeless. And some believe a few million people experience homelessness throughout the year.

Despite this recent downturn in the economy, America still possesses enormous riches. American private wealth, the value of the assets we hold, stands at $48.8 trillion. In simple terms, we have the capacity as a country to end homelessness.

But we don't. Why? The leaders in our country, particularly politicians, just don't have the political will to invest in ending this social enigma.

Here are his five top reasons why homelessness in America is the black sheep of politics:

Can you say "bank"? This is the rapper term for incredible amounts of money. Resolving homelessness is expensive. We all know that the main solution to homelessness is housing, an expensive solution even in this real estate downturn. We are talking billions of dollars that political leaders are not willing to spend, even when experts show it is cheaper to house a homeless person than allowing them to live on the streets using our emergency rooms, paramedics, and law enforcement.

The silent political bloc has no influence. Most homeless people do not vote. Imagine if a politician could rally a block of three million voters. But these voters are not empowered. We all know that political dollars go to the most influential.

I once told the mayor of a popular beach resort that if there were a fire and hundreds of homes burned down, he and his City Council would do everything, and spend anything, to house his upwardly mobile now-homeless citizens. But there is no such political will to house the hundreds of homeless people who flock to his tourist attraction. He agreed.

No instant solutions. Even if political leaders were willing to invest billions of dollars, the construction of hundreds of thousands, if not millions of housing units won't be accomplished in one or two political terms. The next generation of leaders will get the credit. Political leaders need to show solutions within their term of office.

Resolving homelessness is a bad sound bite. In this day and age of CNN, MTV, and Apple commercials, whoever can market the best 30-second sound bite attracts the most money and attention. The reasons and solutions to personal homelessness are complicated. It is like describing why your wayward son is not living in that perfect American family behind that white picketed fence home.

How do you describe and explain the solutions to domestic violence, post-traumatic stress syndrome, substance abuse, and/or mental health disease in mere seconds? It is much easier to promote an anti-drug campaign with, "Just say no." Or an educational campaign with, "No child left behind."

whymaslow.com

Finger pointing is less expensive. No one wants to take the blame for social ills. It means political death. Blaming the one who is homeless is so much more convenient. Homeless people are lazy, crazy, and are choosing to live on the streets, they say. Who wants to invest money and political capital in them?

No wonder why we allow hundreds of thousands of our fellow citizens to languish on our streets like this is some two-bit Third World nation. It is much easier to just ignore them.[xvii]

5

Health, Family, Social Stability

The roots of current healthcare systems can be traced back to the Middle Age guilds, as back then guild members shared funds for supporting elderly and sick people, and also to the charity organizations constituted alongside churches. But the first modern health care system was created in XX-th century in Germany, by Chancellor Bismarck, with the purpose of providing healthcare services to industrial workers, through a health insurance scheme. In XX-th century England, at the initiative of David Lloyd George, a compulsory insurance system was implemented for miners. In the USA, Henry Kaiser developed the first social health insurance plan, having today a few million insured people. After the Second World War, the National Health System (NHS) appeared in Great Britain, organized by Lord Beveridge and in the USSR appeared the Semashko soviet system, a centralized, state-owned system, based on socialist principles.

Do political ideologies exert an influence over the way healthcare systems are organized and function? Some authors call it the 'ideological factor', expressing the dominant conception over the role and importance of different actors in the social and economic structure of a state.

These approaches can be classified in three major trends: conservative, liberal and radical.

- **The conservative** approach is based on the 'equality in front of the law' principle and implies government involvement only with the purpose of law enforcement. Planning is rejected; the market is free and acts upon demand and supply.
- **The liberal** approach is based on the 'equality of chances' principle that cannot be let in the hands of free market. State intervention is accepted, with the purpose of accomplishing improvements in population health status. In practical terms, this principle inspires those states that either adopted a national healthcare system, or a system with state-controlled health insurance agencies.
- **The radical** approach is based on 'equality of results' principle. State intervention is allowed, no matter how massive it would be. Centralized planning and pulling up all resources by the state are among the characteristics of this approach.

Regarding health care system organization, two different models have been imposed at the international level, and they represent the source of inspiration for most European countries.

The first of the two systems is adopted by Great Britain and Sweden, known as the '**Beveridge system**' after its founder and it is a system accessible to everyone, being financed through fees and taxes. The total amount of allowance does not depend on prior salary and healthcare is guaranteed to all without a prior contribution.

System management is carried out by a professional administration, under the control of Parliament. British model inspired more or less countries such as Italy, Spain, Greece and Portugal.

The Second type of system that has been imposed in Germany, but also in Benelux countries, is the '**Bismarck system**', named after the German Chancellor, which created this model. Contributions, established according to work, are managed by independent Insurance Funds chosen by the contributor. The system is not managed by the state; it does not depend on Parliament, but being ruled by the trade-unionists, who negotiate with the doctors. Healthcare is agreed on a contract basis, signed between medical professions and Health Insurance Funds, the latter representing the interest of the contributors.

In 2006, a group of American researchers led by prof. V. Navaro, have published an analysis through which they searched for the connection between politics and policies, and then, their connection to healthcare systems in Europe and North America, between 1950-2000. The conclusion was that countries governed by political parties of egalitarian views have the tendency to implement redistributive policies. The four political traditions were defined as: social democratic, Christian-democratic (conservative), liberal, conservative-authoritarian (dictatorships).

Thereby, countries governed by social-democratic parties during most of the studied period, such as Sweden (45 years), Norway (39 years), Denmark (35 years), Finland (32 years) and Austria (31 years) implemented policies favorable to redistribution, universal health coverage and social benefits for all the citizens, family oriented services such as homecare or child care, with a social expenditure of almost 30% of GDP and a public funds health budget of 7,2% of GDP. Likewise, there were introduced supporting policies for women health and welfare, such as unemployment compensation benefits for single mothers.

Countries governed by Christian-democratic parties, such as Italy and Holland (41 years each), West Germany (37 years), Belgium (35 years), France (29 years), were supporting less redistributive policies. Although these countries also promoted health policies with universal coverage, they did not implement family support policies such as homecare or children care.

Public expenditure was noticeably lower, with an average social expenditure of 28% of GDP and 6,4% of GDP for public health expenditures.

Countries mostly governed by liberal or conservative liberal parties – Great Britain (36 years), Ireland (35 years), Canada (31 years), USA (28 years), did not promote universal social services, except for universal healthcare, which was promoted in all the above countries except for US, with a public expenditure of 24% of GDP for social services and of 5,8% of GDP for health.

Countries led by dictatorships, such as Spain (25 years), Portugal (24 years), or by authoritative regimes – Greece (9 years), had an underdeveloped welfare state, with weak public transfers and poor public services. Average public expenditures were 14% of GDP, with 4,8% of GDP for health. Regarding the direct connection between policies and health indicators, 'it has been observed that redistributive policies seem to account for infantile mortality rate reduction and, to a lesser degree, for life expectancy increase'. We should note that a connection between politics, policies and healthcare systems can only be taken into consideration if the analysis refers to a long, cumulative period of political parties' governance. Another conclusion was that the connection between ideologies and public policies implementation is a complex one, much more so as, it has been observed during last 30 years, that many of those countries governed by social-democratic parties inclined to implement neo-liberal policies.[xviii]

BAMBRA Clare, FOX Debbie, SCOTT-SAMUEL Alex, in their online publication: **"Towards a politics of health"**, determine that:

It is time that the implicit and sometimes explicit but unstated politics within and surrounding health were more widely acknowledged. Health, like almost all other aspects of human life, is political in numerous ways:

- Health is political because, like any other resource or commodity under a neo-liberal economic system, some social groups have more of it than others.

- Health is political because its social determinants are amenable to political interventions and are thereby dependent on political action (or more usually, inaction).

- Health is political because the right to 'a standard of living adequate for health and well-being' (United Nations, 1948) is, or should be, an aspect of citizenship and a human right.

Ultimately, health is political because power is exercised over it as part of a wider economic, social and political system.

Changing this system requires political awareness and political struggle.

Health inequalities

Evidence that the most powerful determinants of health in modern populations are social, economic and cultural (Doyal and Pennell, 1979; Townsend and Davidson, 1992; Whitehead, 1992; Blane et al., 1996; Acheson, 1998) comes from a wide range of sources and is also, to some extent, acknowledged by governments and international agencies (Townsend and Davidson, 1992; Acheson, 1998; Department of Health, 1998; Social Exclusion Unit, 1998). Yet inequalities in health continue, within countries (on the basis of socio-economic class, gender or ethnicity) and between them (in terms of wealth and resources) (Davey Smith et al., 2002; Donkn et al., 2002).

How these inequalities in health are approached by society is highly political: are health inequalities to be accepted as 'natural' and inevitable results of individual differences both in respect of genetics and the silent hand of the economic market, or are they social and economic abhorrence that need to be tackled by a modern state and a humane society (Adams et al., 2002)? Underpinning these different approaches to health inequalities are not only divergent views of what is scientifically or economically possible, but also differing political and ideological opinions about what is desirable.

Health determinants

Causes of, and genetic predispositions to ill-health are becoming increasingly well understood. However, it is evident that in most cases, environmental triggers are equally if not more important and that the major determinants of health or ill-health are inextricably linked to social and economic context (Acheson, 1998; Marmot and Wilkinson, 2001). Factors such as housing, income and employment—indeed many of the issues that dominate political life—are key determinants of our health and well-being. Similarly, many of the major determinants of health inequalities lie outside the health sector and therefore require non-health sector policies to tackle them (Townsend and Davidson, 1992; Acheson, 1998; Whitehead et al., 2000). Recent acknowledgements of the importance of the social determinants of health are welcome but fail to seriously address the underlying political determinants of health and health inequity.

Citizenship

Citizenship is 'a status bestowed on those who are full members of a community. All who possess the status are equal with respect to the rights and duties with which the status is endowed' (Marshall, 1963). There are three types of citizenship rights: civil, political and social. Health, or the 'right to a standard of living adequate for health and well-being' (United Nations, 1948; International Forum for the Defense of the Health of People, 2002), is an important social citizenship right. These citizenship rights were only gained as a result of extensive political and social struggle during Western industrialization and the development of capitalism (Marshall, 1963). However, despite their parallel development, the relationship between capitalism and citizenship is not an easy or 'natural' one (Marshall, 1963). Health is a strong example of this tense relationship as under a capitalist economic system health is, like everything else, commoditized. Commoditization is 'the process whereby everything becomes identifiable and valued according to its relative desirability within the economic market (of production and consumption)' (de Viggiani, 1997). Health became extensively commoditized during the industrial revolution as workers became entirely dependent upon the market for their survival (Esping-Andersen, 1990). In the 20th century, the introduction of social citizenship, which entailed an entitlement to health and social welfare, brought about a 'loosening' of the pure commodity status of health. The welfare state decommoditized health because certain health services and a certain standard of living became a right of citizenship.

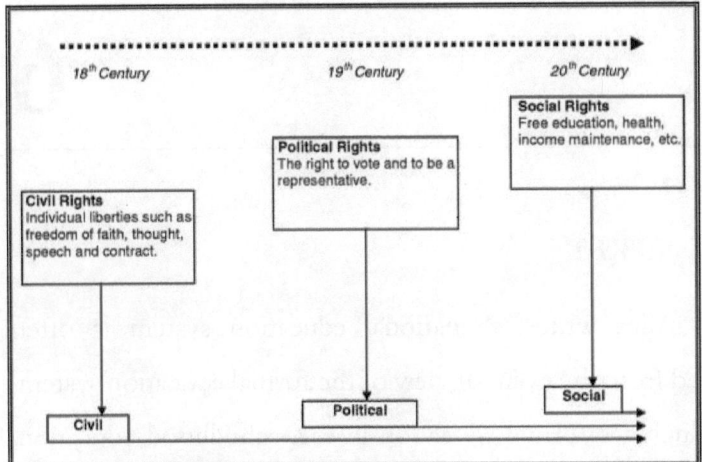

The historical development of citizenship (adapted from Marshall, 1963).

In short, capitalism and citizenship represent very different values: the former, inequality and the latter, equality. This tension means that the implementation of the right to health, despite its position in social citizenship and in the UN Universal Declaration of Human Rights, will for the foreseeable future require continuing political struggle.[xix]

6

Education

Sarah Alice writes: A national education system is often defined from the point of view of the formal education system. This includes formal education in early childhood education, primary education, secondary education, higher education and university education. Subsets of informal and non-formal education are often considered part of formal education and, if they are not completely ignored, receive little attention. However, it is important that the national education system fully integrates all subsets of the education system, namely formal, informal and non-formal education.

Our perceptions of child development and learning styles change as new studies and findings present evidence to confirm or modify one theory or another. The practices with respect to education in the United States have changed from one generation to another. Evolution is natural and continues as research and empirical studies continue.

To what extent does national education policy make a difference in the classroom and how much does national policy drive educational policy in the United States, where schools, curricula, and teaching have been controlled at the local and state levels? since the dawn of public schools?

The political philosophy that controls the government of a country often has its inevitable impact on education. The political factor dictates the type of administration that the educational system will have. Behind the characteristics of the education system and how it works. *For example, the fundamental ideas of socialism as political philosophy referred to the exploitation of labor by capital and this gave rise to the mass of the class.* As a political philosophy, socialism recognizes property as the basis of the economic structure of the state that results in the concentration of civil and legal power in the hands of the propertied class. Socialism advocates the nationalization of the means of production where the owners of the means of production do not work and the workers who produce do not own anything. A change of such social order can only be achieved with educational reform. This would be through a state mechanism with full control of education and the curriculum, and this means that citizens must be trained by the state, for the state, and in state institutions. In such cases, the details of the curriculum are often decided by state authorities and involve the functional training of citizens. The curriculum may also include scientific training for social use purposes.

Good examples of countries that have introduced a socialist education system are Mexico, Bulgaria, and Cuba. The common characteristics of its educational system include the monopoly of state control over education, secularism, physical and military training, political indoctrination inside and outside the school and also a greater emphasis on science subjects. In these states, the freedom of the people and the idea of tolerance are not accepted. Unlike these countries, France has a centralized education system based on its political philosophy. In France, everything related to education is controlled from the center (metropolis) which is the central government. In the case of EE. In the United States and Japan, their education systems are highly decentralized and often based on the democratic influence and capitalist political philosophy of these countries.

There is also a close relationship between the national character and the national education system. For example, the national character of the United States is democratic, so that its educational system is democratic in most aspects. Nationalism also as a political ideology influences the educational system of a country. Nationalism could be defined as a psychological feeling within a group that believes to have a common vision, and traditions based on the myth of the common ancestor. These common ancestors include race, language, religion, and territory and often strengthen the awareness of nationality. The racial aspect that is often within the political ideology of a country can play an important role in determining the characteristics of the educational system. The race refers to a tribe, a nation or a group of nations. The modern population includes people of different racial origins. The British colonial policy was based on the principle of decentralization and the construction of a community of nations, each of which should be free to develop its own national culture and character. Therefore, there is a close relationship between the national character and the national education system and the first has been universally accepted as an important base of the national education system. Therefore, the policy system of a country is closely related to its educational program.[xx]

How Education and Training Affect the Economy

Brent Radcliffe in his article published in Investopedia states the following: Globalization and international trade require countries and their economies to compete with each other. Economically successful countries will hold competitive and comparative advantages over other economies, though a single country rarely specializes in a particular industry. This means the country's economy will include various industries with different advantages and disadvantages in the global marketplace. The education and training of a country's workers is a major factor in determining just how well the country's economy will do.

A successful economy has a workforce capable of operating industries at a level where it holds a competitive advantage over the economies of other countries. To achieve this, nations may try incentivizing training through tax breaks and write-offs, providing facilities to train workers, or a variety of other means designed to create a more skilled workforce. While it is unlikely an economy will hold a competitive advantage in all industries, it can focus on a number of industries in which skilled professionals are more readily trained.

Differences in training levels have been cited as a significant factor separating developed and developing countries. Although other factors are certainly in play, such as geography and available resources, having better-trained workers creates spillovers and externalities. For example, similar businesses may cluster in the same geographic region because of the availability of skilled workers (e.g. Silicon Valley).

Employers want workers who are productive and require less management. Employers must consider many factors when deciding whether or not to pay for employee training.

- Will the training program increase the productivity of the workers?
- Will the increase in productivity warrant the cost of paying for all or part of the training program?

- If the employer pays for training, will the employee leave the company for a competitor after the training program is complete?
- Will the newly trained worker be able to command a higher wage? Will the worker see an increase in his or her bargaining power?

While employers should be wary about newly trained workers leaving, many employers require workers to continue with the firm for a certain amount of time in exchange for the company paying for training.

Businesses may also face employees who are unwilling to accept training. This can happen in industries dominated by unions since increased job security could make it more difficult to hire trained professionals or fire less-trained employees. However, unions may also negotiate with employers to ensure their members are better trained and thus more productive, which reduces the likelihood of jobs being shifted overseas.

Workers increase their earning potential by developing and refining their capabilities. The more they know about a particular job's function, or the more they understand a particular industry, the more valuable they become to an employer. Employees want to learn advanced techniques or new skills to vie for a higher wage. Usually, workers can expect their wages to increase at a smaller percentage than the productivity gains by employers. The worker must consider a number of factors when deciding whether to enter a training program:

How much extra productivity would he or she expect to gain?

- What is the cost of the training program? Will the worker see a wage increase that would warrant the cost of the program?
- What is the labor market like for a better-trained professional? Is the market significantly saturated with trained labor already?

Some employers pay for all or a portion of the expense of a program, but this is not always the case. In fact, the worker may lose wages if the program prevents him or her from working.

Many countries have placed greater emphasis on developing an education system that can produce workers able to function in new industries, such as those in the fields of technology and science. This is partly because older industries in developed economies were becoming less competitive, and thus were less likely to continue dominating the industrial landscape. Also, a movement to improve the basic education of the population emerged, with a growing belief that all people had the right to an education.

When economists speak of "education," the focus is not strictly on workers obtaining college degrees. Education is often broken into specific levels:

- Primary – elementary school in the U.S.
- Secondary – middle school, high school, and preparatory school
- Post-secondary – university, community college, vocational schools

A country's economy becomes more productive as the proportion of educated workers increases since educated workers can more efficiently carry out tasks that require literacy and critical thinking. However, obtaining a higher level of education also carries a cost. A country doesn't have to provide an extensive network of colleges or universities to benefit from education; it can provide basic literacy programs and still see economic improvements.

Countries with a greater portion of their population attending and graduating from schools see faster economic growth than countries with less educated workers. As a result, many countries provide funding for primary and secondary education to improve economic performance. In this sense, education is an investment in human capital, similar to an investment in better equipment. According to UNESCO and the United Nations Human Development Programme, the ratio of the number of children of official secondary school age enrolled in school to the number of children of official secondary school age in the population (referred to as the enrollment ratio), is higher in developed nations than it is in developing ones. This differs from education spending as a percentage of GDP, which does not always correlate strongly with how educated a country's population is. Therefore, a country spending a high proportion of its GDP on education does not necessarily make the country's population more educated.[xxi]

Barriers to Education around the World

A work by Phineas Rueckert, published on January 23, 2018, gives a light about the Barriers to Education around the World:

A lack of funding for education

While the Global Partnership for Education is helping many developing countries to increase their own domestic financing for education, global donor support for education is decreasing at an alarming rate. The amount of total aid that's allocated to education has decreased in each of the past six years, and education aid is 4% lower than it was in 2009. This is creating a global funding crisis that is having serious consequences on countries' ability to get children into school and learning.

Money isn't everything, but it is a key foundation for a successful education system.

The Global Partnership is aiming to raise $3.1 billion in new investment from donor countries into the GPE fund, as well as increases in other aid to education, and is also asking developing country partners to pledge increases in their own domestic financing.

Having no teacher, or having an untrained teacher

What's the number one thing any child needs to be able to learn? A teacher, of course.

We're facing multiple challenges when it comes to teachers. Not only are there not enough teachers globally to achieve universal primary education (let alone secondary), but many of the teachers that are currently working are also untrained, leading to children failing to learn the basics, such as math and language skills. Globally, the UN estimates that 69 million new teachers are required to achieve universal primary and secondary education by 2030. Meanwhile, in one out of three countries, less than three-quarters of teachers are trained to national standards.

In 2016 alone, the Global Partnership for Education helped to train 238,000 teachers worldwide. With a successful replenishment, GPE can make teacher recruitment and training a top global priority for delivering quality education for all.

No classroom

This seems like a pretty obvious one – if you don't have a classroom, you don't really have much of a chance of getting a decent education. But again, that's a reality for millions of children worldwide. Children in many countries in Sub-Saharan Africa are often squeezed into overcrowded classrooms, classrooms that are falling apart, or are learning outside.

In Malawi, for example, there are 130 children per classroom in grade 1 on average. It's not just a lack of classrooms that's the problem, but also all the basic facilities you would expect a school to have – like running water and toilets.

In Chad, only one in seven schools has potable water, and just one in four has a toilet; moreover, only one-third of the toilets that do exist are for girls only – a real disincentive and barrier for girls to come to school.

Since 2011 funding from the Global Partnership for Education has helped to build or rehabilitate 53,000 classrooms. With an additional $3.1 billion, GPE could help build an additional 23,800 classrooms, while training over 1.7 million teachers, among other things.

A lack of learning materials

Outdated and worn-out textbooks are often shared by six or more students in many parts of the world. In Tanzania, for example, only 3.5% of all grades 6 pupils had sole use of a reading textbook. In Cameroon, there are 11 primary school students for every reading textbook and 13 for every mathematics textbook in grade 2. Workbooks, exercise sheets, readers and other core materials to help students learn their lessons are in short supply. Teachers also need materials to help prepare their lessons, share with their students, and guide their lessons.

For example, GPE funding helped deliver 146 million textbooks to all primary and secondary school students in Ethiopia, increasing access to quality services in an estimated 40,000 schools.

The exclusion of children with disabilities

Despite the fact that education is a universal human right, being denied access to school is common for the world's 93 million children with disabilities. In some of the world's poorest countries, up to 95% of children with disabilities are out of school. A combination of discrimination, lack of training in inclusive teaching methods among teachers, and a straightforward lack of disabled accessible schools leave this group uniquely vulnerable to being denied their right to education.

Children with disabilities are one of the Global Partnership for Education's priorities. With a successful replenishment, the GPE will be able to work with its more than 60 developing country partners to promote inclusive education.

The GPE already has a proven track record in this capacity. For example, at the Daerit Elementary School in Asmara, Eritrea, children are taught that, "All children can learn." And with funds from GPE, the school is pioneering inclusive education in the country.

Being the 'wrong' gender

Put simply, gender is one of the biggest reasons why children are denied an education. Despite recent advances in girls' education, a generation of young women has been left behind. Over 130 million young women around the world are not currently enrolled in school. At least one in five adolescent girls around the world is denied an education by the daily realities of poverty, conflict and discrimination.

Poverty forces many families to choose which of their children to send to school. Girls often miss out due to the belief that there's less value in educating a girl than a boy. Instead, they are sent to work or made to stay at home to look after siblings and work on household chores. Girls also miss days of school every year or are too embarrassed to participate in class, because they don't have appropriate menstrual hygiene education or toilet facilities at their school to manage their period in privacy and with dignity.

Ensuring girls can access and complete a quality education is a top priority for the Global Partnership for Education. Since its inception, GPE has helped 38 million additional girls go to school. Sixty-four percent of the developing countries GPE supports and works with succeeded in getting equal numbers of girls and boys to complete primary school in 2015. GPE funds have also resulted in better sanitary facilities, like toilet blocks and gender separated toilets worldwide. With a successful replenishment, GPE could get an additional 9.4 million girls in school by 2020.

Living in a country in conflict or at risk of conflict

There are many casualties of any war, and education systems are often destroyed. While this may seem obvious, the impact of conflict cannot be overstated. In 2017, around 50 million children were living in countries affected by conflicts, with 27 million of them out of school, according to UNICEF. Conflict prevents governments from functioning, teachers and students often flee their homes, and continuity of learning is greatly disrupted. In total, 75 million children have had their education disrupted by conflict or crisis, including natural disasters that destroy schools and the environment around them. Worryingly, education has thus far been a very low priority in humanitarian aid to countries in conflict – and less than 3% of global humanitarian assistance was allocated to education in 2016.

Since its establishment, the Global Partnership for Education has committed nearly half of all its grants ($2.3 billion) to conflict-affected and fragile states. Nearly half of all GPE funded countries classify as either "fragile" or "affected by conflict." The Global Partnership is also right now looking at how to further improve its operations to accelerate support to countries in emergencies or early recovery situations.

Distance from home to school

For many children around the world, a walk to school of up to three hours in each direction is common. This is just too much for many children, particularly those children with a disability, those suffering from malnutrition or illness, or those who are required to work around the household. Imagine having to set off for school, hungry, at 5 a.m. every day, not to return until 7pm. Many children, especially girls, are also vulnerable to violence on their long and hazardous journeys to and from school.

By investing in new schools, more schools, the Global Partnership for Education is helping to reduce the distances children have to travel to get to school for a decent education. With pledges of support from donors, the GPE can help ensure no child has to endure such long journeys just to fulfill their basic right to education.

Hunger and poor nutrition.

The impact of hunger on education systems is gravely underreported. Being severely malnourished, to the point it impacts on brain development, can be the same as losing four grades of schooling. Around 171 million children in developing countries are stunted by hunger by the time they reach age 5. Stunting can affect a child's cognitive abilities as well as their focus and concentration in school. As a result, stunted children are 19% less likely to be able to read by age eight. Conversely, good nutrition can be crucial preparation for good learning.

The Global Partnership for Education seeks to address national priorities as decided by developing country governments themselves. Where malnutrition is a major concern, the GPE is stepping in to address the problem.

For instance, in Lao People's Democratic Republic, an innovative School Meals Program funded by GPE is addressing students' nutritional deficits as well as promoting self-reliance, community ownership, and sustainability through integrated local food production and the active involvement of community members. As a result, Lao PDR has seen increased school enrollment (especially for girls), improved nutritional status, reduced household expenses, and stronger student-teacher-parent and community relations.

The expense of education

The Universal Declaration of Human Rights makes clear that every child has the right to a free basic education, so that poverty and lack of money should not be a barrier to schooling. In many developing countries, over the last decades governments have announced the abolition of school fees and as a result, seen impressive increases in the number of children going to school.

But for many of the poorest families, school remains too expensive, and children are forced to stay at home doing chores or work themselves. Families remain locked in a cycle of poverty that goes on for generations. In many countries in Africa, while education is theoretically free, in practice 'informal fees' see parents forced to pay for 'compulsory items' like uniforms, books, pens, extra lessons, exam fees or funds to support the school buildings. In other places, the lack of functioning public (government) schools means that parents have no choice but to send their children to private schools that, even if they are 'low fee', are unaffordable for the poorest families who risk making themselves destitute in their efforts to get their children better lives through education.[xxii]

PART III. GOVERNMENTS AND THE HIERARCHY OF NEEDS

7

Keep them in their primitive stage!

"Fundamentally, poverty is a denial of choices and opportunities, a violation of human dignity. It means lack of basic capacity to participate effectively in society. It means not having enough to feed and clothe a family, not having a school or clinic to go to, not having the land on which to grow one's food or a job to earn one's living, not having access to credit. It means insecurity, powerlessness and exclusion of individuals, households and communities. It means susceptibility to violence, and it often implies living on marginal or fragile environments, without access to clean water or sanitation" (UN Statement, June 1998 – signed by the heads of all UN agencies)

A study, by Dr. David Gordon[xxiii], proposes Indicators to Measure Poverty, based on Deprivation of Human Needs, which can be conceptualized as a continuum which ranges from no deprivation through mild, moderate and severe deprivation to extreme deprivation.

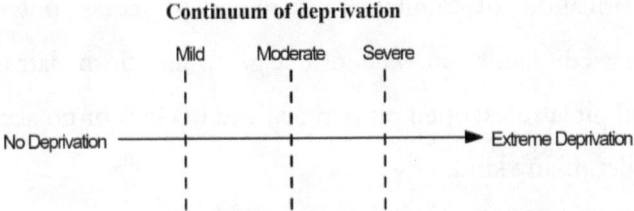

In order to measure absolute poverty amongst children, it is necessary to define the threshold measures of severe deprivation of basic human need for:

1. Food
2. Safe drinking water
3. Sanitation facilities
4. Health
5. Shelter
6. Education
7. Information
8. Access to services

Proposed Operational Definitions of Deprivation of Basic Human Need for Youth

1) Food Deprivation– Body Mass Index of 18.5 or below (underweight).

2) Water Deprivation - access only to unimproved source such as open wells, open springs or surface water or who have to walk for more than 15 minutes to their water source (30 minutes round-trip).

3) Deprivation of Sanitation Facilities – access only to unimproved sanitation facilities e.g.: pour flush latrines; covered pit latrines; open pit latrines; and buckets or no access to a toilet of any kind.

4) Health Deprivation – Women who did not receive treatment for a recent serious illness or who did not receive the minimum standard of antenatal care from a person trained in midwifery or who do not know that a healthy person can transmit HIV/AIDS or who do not know that using a condom during sex can prevent HIV/AIDS transmission. Men who did not receive treatment for a recent serious illness or who do not know that a healthy person can transmit HIV/AIDS or that using a condom during sex can prevent HIV/AIDS transmission.

5) Shelter Deprivation – living in dwellings with 3 or more people per room (overcrowding) or in a house with no flooring (e.g. a mud floor) or inadequate roofing (e.g. natural roofing materials)

6) Education Deprivation – youth who did not complete primary school or who are illiterate

7) Information Deprivation – no access to a radio or television (i.e. broadcast media) at home.

The Poverty threshold is equal to 2 or more deprivations of basic human need.

whymaslow.com

Again, when we take a second look at the Hierarchies Pyramid, we will notice that the first and second stages are directly related to poverty:

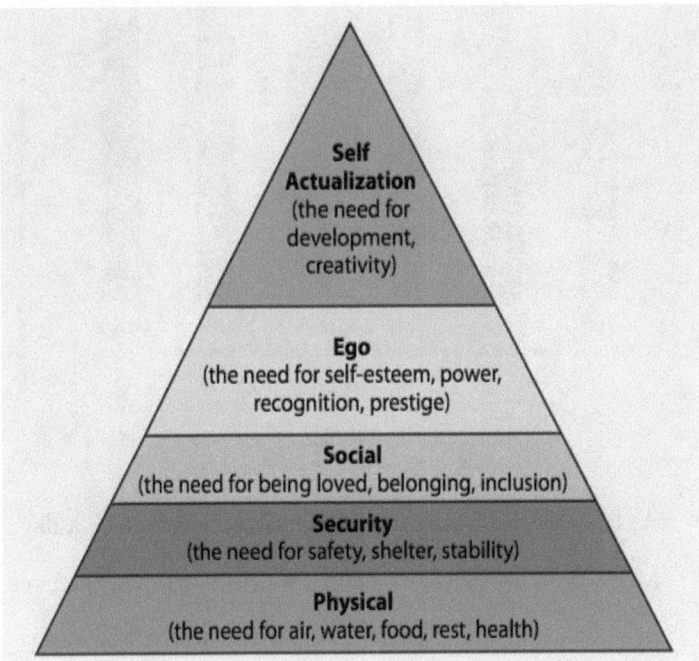

If we check the following facts, collected and published by Anup Shah[xxiv]:

- Almost half the world — over three billion people — live on less than $2.50 a day.

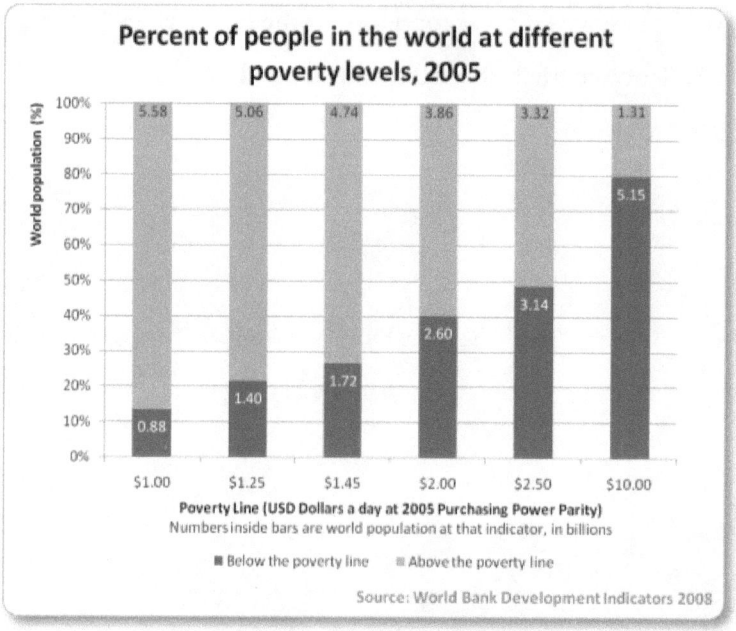

- At least 80% of humanity lives on less than $10 a day.
- More than 80 percent of the world's population lives in countries where income differentials are widening.
- The poorest 40 percent of the world's population accounts for 5 percent of global income.
- The richest 20 percent accounts for three-quarters of the world's income.
- According to UNICEF, 22,000 children die each day due to poverty. And they die quietly in some of the poorest villages on earth, far removed from the scrutiny and the conscience of the world. Being meek

and weak in life makes these dying multitudes even more invisible in death.

- Around 27-28 percent of all children in developing countries are estimated to be underweight or stunted. The two regions that account for the bulk of the deficit are South Asia and sub-Saharan Africa.

If current trends continue, the Millennium Development Goals target of halving the proportion of underweight children will be missed by 30 million children, largely because of slow progress in Southern Asia and sub-Saharan Africa.

- Based on enrollment data, about 72 million children of primary school age in the developing world were not in school in 2005; 57 per cent of them were girls. And these are regarded as optimistic numbers.

- Nearly a billion people entered the 21st century unable to read a book or sign their names.

- Less than one per cent of what the world spent every year on weapons was needed to put every child into school by the year 2000 and yet it didn't happen.

- Infectious diseases continue to blight the lives of the poor across the world. An estimated 40 million people are living with HIV/AIDS, with 3 million deaths in 2004. Every year there are 350–500 million cases of malaria, with 1 million fatalities: Africa accounts for 90 percent of malarial deaths and African children account for over 80 percent of malaria victims worldwide.

Water problems affect half of humanity:

- Some 1.1 billion people in developing countries have inadequate access to water, and 2.6 billion lack basic sanitation.
- Almost two in three people lacking access to clean water survive on less than $2 a day, with one in three living on less than $1 a day.
- More than 660 million people without sanitation live on less than $2 a day, and more than 385 million on less than $1 a day.
- Access to piped water into the household averages about 85% for the wealthiest 20% of the population, compared with 25% for the poorest 20%.
- 1.8 billion people who have access to a water source within 1 kilometer, but not in their house or yard, consume around 20 liters per day. In the United Kingdom the average person uses more than 50 liters of water a day flushing toilets (where average daily water usage is about 150 liters a day. The highest average water use in the world is in the US, at 600 liters day.)

- Some 1.8 million child deaths each year as a result of diarrhea
- The loss of 443 million school days each year from water-related illness.
- Close to half of all people in developing countries suffer at any given time from a health problem caused by water and sanitation deficits.
- Millions of women spending several hours a day collecting water.

To these human costs can be added the massive economic waste associated with the water and sanitation deficit.... The costs associated with health spending, productivity losses and labor diversions ... are greatest in some of the poorest countries. Sub-Saharan Africa loses about 5% of GDP, or some $28.4 billion annually, a figure that exceeds total aid flows and debt relief to the region in 2003.

Number of children in the world

2.2 billion

Number in poverty:

1 billion (every second child)

Shelter, safe water and health

For the 1.9 billion children from the developing world, there are:

- 640 million without adequate shelter (1 in 3)

- 400 million with no access to safe water (1 in 5)
- 270 million with no access to health services (1 in 7)

Children out of education worldwide

121 million

Survival for children

- Worldwide, 10.6 million died in 2003 before they reached the age of 5 (same as children population in France, Germany, Greece and Italy)
- 1.4 million die each year from lack of access to safe drinking water and adequate sanitation.

Health of children

- Worldwide, 2.2 million children die each year because they are not immunized.
- 15 million children orphaned due to HIV/AIDS (similar to the total children population in Germany or United Kingdom)

Rural areas account for three in every four people living on less than US$1 a day and a similar share of the world population suffering from malnutrition. However, urbanization is not synonymous with human progress. Urban slum growth is outpacing urban growth by a wide margin.

- Approximately half the world's population now live in cities and towns. In 2005, one out of three urban dwellers (approximately 1 billion people) were living in slum conditions.

- In developing countries some 2.5 billion people are forced to rely on biomass—fuel wood, charcoal and animal dung—to meet their energy needs for cooking. In sub-Saharan Africa, over 80 percent of the population depends on traditional biomass for cooking, as do over half of the populations of India and China.

- Indoor air pollution resulting from the use of solid fuels [by poorer segments of society] is a major killer. It claims the lives of 1.5 million people each year, more than half of them below the age of five: that is 4000 deaths a day. To put this number in context, it exceeds total deaths from malaria and rivals the number of deaths from tuberculosis.

In 2005, the wealthiest 20% of the world accounted for 76.6% of total private consumption. The poorest fifth just 1.5%

If the Governments in Association with Industry Leaders/Owners manage the wealth and Natural Resources around the world, then who is responsible of keeping the 80% of the Population dying of starvation and diseases on the two basic stages of the Maslow Pyramid of Needs?

whymaslow.com

THE AUTHOR

Juan Ramon Rodulfo Moya, **Defined by Nature**: Inhabitant of Planet Earth, Human, Son of Eladio Rodulfo and Briceida Moya, Brother of Gabriela, Gustavo and Katiuska, Father of Gabriel and Sofia; **Defined by society**: Venezuelan Citizen (Limited Human Rights by default), Friend of many, enemy of few, Neighbor, Student/Teacher/Student, Worker/Supervisor/Manager/Leader/Worker, Husband of K/Ex-Husband of K/Husband of Y; **Defined by the U.S. Immigration Office**: Legal Alien; **Classroom studies**: Master's Degree in Human Resource Management, English, Mandarin Chinese; **Real-World Studies**: Human Behavior; **Home Studios**: SEO Webmaster, Graphic Design, Application and Website Development, Internet and Social Media Marketing, Video Production, YouTube Branding, Part 107 Commercial Drone Pilot, Import-Export, Affiliate Marketing, Cooking, Laundry, Home Cleaning; **Work experience**: Public-Private-Entrepreneurial Sectors; **Other definitions:** Bitcoin Evangelist, Defender of Human Rights, Peace and Love.

whymaslow.com

Publications:

Books:

- Why Maslow: How to use his theory to stay in Power Forever (EN/SP)

- Asylum Seekers (EN/SP)

- Manual for Gorillas: 9 Rules to be the "Fer-pect" Dictator (EN/SP)

- Why you must Play the Lottery (EN/SP); Para Español Oprima #2: Speaking Spanish in Times of Xenophobia (EN/SP)

- Cause of Death: IGNORANCE | Human Behavior in Times of PANIC (EN/SP)

- Politics explained for Millennials, GENs XYZ and future generations (EN/SP)

- Las cenizas del Ejército Libertador (EN/SP)

- Remain Silent: The only right we have. The legal Aliens (EN/SP)

- Fortune Cookie Coaching 88 Motivational Tips Made Of Fortune Cookies, Vol I (EN)

Blogs:

Noticias de Nueva Esparta, Ubuntu Café, Coffee Secrets, Guaripete Pro, Rodulfox, Red Wasp Drone, Barista Pro, Gorila Travel, Fortune Cookie Coach, All Books, Vicky Toys.

whymaslow.com

Audiovisual Productions:

Podcasts:
Ubuntu Cafe | Vicky Erotic Tales | Fortune Cookie Coach | All Books, available at: juanrodulfo.com/podcasts

Music:
Albums: Margarita | Race to Extinction | Relaxed Panda | Amazonia | Cassiopeia | Caracas | Arcoiris Musical | Close Your Eyes, Daintree, He'e nalu, disponibles en: juanrodulfo.com/music

Photography & Video:
On sale at Adobe Stock, iStock, Shutterstock, and Veectezy, available at: juanrodulfo.com/gallery

Social Media Profiles:

Twitter / FB / Instagram / TikTok/ VK / Linkedin / Sina Weibo: **@rodulfox**

Google Author: https://g.co/kgs/grjtN5
Google Artist: https://g.co/kgs/H7Fiqg
Twitter: https://twitter.com/rodulfox
Facebook: https://facebook.com/rodulfox
LinkedIn: https://www.linkedin.com/in/rodulfox
Instagram: https://www.instagram.com/rodulfox/
VK: https://vk.com/rodulfox

TikTok: https://www.tiktok.com/@rodulfox

TradingView: https://www.tradingview.com/u/rodulfox/

Endnotes

[i] I refer to Political Forces, not only to the Government of Venezuela converted into a Dictatorship hidden behind a pseudo democracy and the PSUV Party, but to Private Capital and other World Governments with Interests in that land named Venezuela.

[ii] First World but rolling back to Second? Third?...

[iii] Bilash Olenka, Maslow's Hierarchy of Needs, (Last Modified June 2009), Retrieved October 30, 2018, from: https://sites.educ.ualberta.ca/staff/olenka.bilash/Best%20of%20Bilash/maslowshierarchy.html

[iv] Boeree C. George, ABRAHAM MASLOW 1908-1970, (2006), Retrieved October 30, 2018, from: http://webspace.ship.edu/cgboer/maslow.html

[v] Boeree C. George, Abraham Maslow 1908-1970, (2006), Retrieved October 30, 2018, from: http://webspace.ship.edu/cgboer/maslow.html

[vi] McLeod Saul, Maslow Hierarchy of needs, (updated 2018), Retrieved October 30, 2018, from: https://www.simplypsychology.org/maslow.html

[vii] Burton Neel, Our Hierarchy of Needs True Freedom is a luxury of the mind. Find out why, (May 23, 2012), Retrieved October 30, 2018, from: https://www.psychologytoday.com/us/blog/hide-and-seek/201205/our-hierarchy-needs

[viii] Abulof, U. Soc (2017) 54: 508. https://doi.org/10.1007/s12115-017-0198-6

[ix] Wikipedia, Maslow's Hierarchy of needs, (October 26, 2018), Retrieved October 30, 2018, from: https://en.wikipedia.org/wiki/Maslow%27s_hierarchy_of_needs

[x] McLeod Saul, Maslow Hierarchy of needs, (updated 2018), Retrieved October 30, 2018, from: https://www.simplypsychology.org/maslow.html

[xi] Scott Jeffrey, Decoding Maslow's Human Needs to Understand Your Behavior and Psychological Development, Retrieved October 30, 2018, from: https://scottjeffrey.com/abraham-maslow-hierarchy-of-needs/#A_Practical_Approach_to_Maslows_Hierarchy_of_Needs

[xii] Wikipedia, Food Politics, (September 5, 2018), Retrieved October 30, 2018, from: https://en.wikipedia.org/wiki/Food_politics

[xiii] Wikipedia, Food Security, (October 16, 2018), Retrieved October 30, 2018, from: https://en.wikipedia.org/wiki/Food_security#cite_note-26

[xiv] Vijay K Mago, Hilary K Morden, Charles Fritz, Tiankuang Wu, Sara Namazi, Parastoo Geranmayeh, Rakhi Chattopadhyay, and Vahid Dabbaghian, Analyzing the impact of social factors on homelessness: a

Fuzzy Cognitive Map approach, (August 23, 2013), Retrieved October 30, 2018, from: https://www.ncbi.nlm.nih.gov/pmc/articles/PMC3766254/

[xv] Onn Melanie, The Guardian, Homelessness is not inevitable. It's a political choice made by the UK government, (September 13, 2017), Retrieved October 30, 2018, from: https://www.theguardian.com/housing-network/2017/sep/13/homelessness-not-inevitable-political-choice-uk-government

[xvi] Calterone Williams. Jean, The Politics of Homelessness in the United States, (January 2017, Retrieved October 30, 2018, from: http://www.oxfordhandbooks.com/view/10.1093/oxfordhb/9780199935307.001.0001/oxfordhb-9780199935307-e-153

[xvii] Joel John Roberts, Huffpost, Five Reasons Why Politicians Ignore Homelessness, (October 18, 2010), Retrieved October 30, 2018, from: https://www.huffingtonpost.com/joel-john-roberts/five-reasons-why-politici_b_765353.html

[xviii] BUȘOI Cristian Silviu, Health Systems and the Influence of Political Ideologies, (February 14, 2010), Retrieved October 30, 2018, from: http://journal.managementinhealth.com/index.php/rms/article/viewFile/103/234

[xix] BAMBRA Clare, FOX Debbie, SCOTT-SAMUEL Alex, towards a politics of health, (June 2005), Retrieved October 30, 2018, from: https://academic.oup.com/heapro/article/20/2/187/827479

[xx] ALICE Sarah, Political Factors Affecting Education, (November 3, 2017), Retrieved October 30, 2018, from: http://khaleejmag.com/education/political-factors-affecting-education/

[xxi] RADCLIFFE Brent, How Education and Training Affect the Economy, (March 23, 2018), Retrieved October 30, 2018, from: https://www.investopedia.com/articles/economics/09/education-training-advantages.asp

[xxii] RUECKERT Phineas, 10 Barriers to Education Around the World, (January 24, 2018), Retrieved October 30, 2018, from: https://www.globalcitizen.org/en/content/10-barriers-to-education-around-the-world-2/

[xxiii] GORDON David, Indicators of Poverty & Hunger, (December 2005), Retrieved October 30, 2018, from: https://www.un.org/esa/socdev/unyin/documents/ydiDavidGordon_poverty.pdf

[xxiv] SHAH Anup, Poverty Facts and Stats, (January 7, 2013), Retrieved October 30, 2018, from: http://www.globalissues.org/article/26/poverty-facts-and-stats

www.ingramcontent.com/pod-product-compliance
Lightning Source LLC
LaVergne TN
LVHW042252070526
838201LV00109B/329/J